THE CRAZY PARKING TICKET AWARDS

Crazy Councils, Meter Madness and Traffic Warden Hell

BARRIE SEGAL

COPYRIGHT NOTICE

All Rights Reserved

Barrie Segal has asserted his right under the Copyright, Designs and Patents Act, 1988, to be identified as the author of this work The Crazy Parking Ticket Awards™.

Copyright © 2007 – 2017 Barrie Segal

You may not reproduce, store in a retrieval system, or pass on in any form or by any means, electronic, mechanical, photocopying, recording, scanning, or otherwise, except without the prior written permission of the Author.

Terms and Conditions

The information contained in this guide is for information purposes only, and may not apply to your situation. The author, publisher, distributor and provider provide no warranty about the content or accuracy of the content enclosed. Information contained herein is subjective. Please keep this in mind when reviewing this guide.

The information provided in this guide is provided as is, without warranty or any guarantee of the accuracy of the content or information provided. The buyer takes on full responsibility for use of the information contained in this guide.

Neither the Publisher nor Author shall be liable for any loss of profit or any other damages resulting from use of this guide. All links are for information purposes only. We do not warrant for content, accuracy or any other implied or explicit purpose.

First published in paperback under the title "The Parking Tickets Awards" in 2007 by Portico Books.

*This book is dedicated
to the memory of my mother
Rose Segal z"l (1917–2007)
and my dear friend of 40 years
Tony Bohm z"l (1951–2015)*

Acknowledgements

To my family, who listened tirelessly as I never seemed to stop talking about parking tickets, bus lanes and yellow box junctions. Their encouragement has made this book a reality.

To all motorists who believe in fairness and who have been the victims of unfair, or excessive, parking-ticket fines. Your frustration is shared by us all.

To my dear friend Hugh Moses, the motorist whose fight against his unfair parking tickets ended up in the High Court and gained a massive victory for many thousands of motorists.

To all the wonderful people at the Nightingale Hammerson Charity.

In Memory of

My good friend Christopher (Chris) Evans (1940-2012), journalist, author, publisher and raconteur. The man who introduced me to the expression, "No good deed goes unpunished"

My friend Mike Dickin (1943–2006). Broadcaster, journalist and a true man of the people.

Table of Contents

Introduction to the Second Edition 1
A Brief History of the Parking Ticket 7
A Note on Wardens 9
Crazy Parking Ticket Awards - Winners 11
Permit? What Permit? 13
Don't Park with Animals or Children 23
Crash-Bang-Wallop what a Ticket! 29
Star Parking 35
It's Not Just Cars 43
One Good Deed Deserves a Ticket 53
Crime Doesn't Pay 67
Appeals 83
Wardens 87
In Sickness and in Health 93
Just Bonkers 101
(Un)Common Sense 111
Understand and Deliver 117
Bending the Rules 129
Above the Law 139

Introduction to the Second Edition

In November 2003 I started my website, www.appealnow.com, to help motorists fight unfair parking tickets. Almost immediately, I realised that people didn't fight their unfair tickets – either because they were intimidated by the whole appeal process, believing that they couldn't take on the might and financial resources of the local council – or simply because it was just too much like hard work. People believe, however cynical it may sound, that the law is always weighted against them. And, unfortunately, most of the time they are right. However, it was my hope that my website would help level the playing field.

Slowly but surely, people started to use the website to successfully lodge appeals, the news spread, and my venture became a success.

For years I heard rumours about illegal practices that took place when parking tickets were issued, but nobody had proof. So, I started to investigate. Sure enough I uncovered many parking scams that were inflicted upon, and seriously affected, the honest motorist.

The deeper I delved, the more parking scams I uncovered, and I began to publish them on my website. To date, I have exposed more than seventy-three scams Some scams are so ingenious that I have decided not to publish them lest they become more widespread.

As I kept discovering it wasn't just the fraudsters that are in it for the money; even local councils and parking attendants have gone to extraordinary lengths to issue parking tickets. One council, I discovered, even ran a bonus scheme for parking attendants featuring a £12,000 car as first prize!

It seemed to me that the most effective way to publicise these scams, and often the incredible stupidity of local authorities in enforcing parking regulations, was to offer awards to the craziest, silliest, most bizarre parking tickets. With that, the Crazy Parking Tickets Awards were born and fourteen years later we are still going strong. The stories of the (un)lucky 'winners' and runners-up are all included in this book.

It has become apparent that as more and more councils take over responsibility for parking enforcement from the police, a more cavalier approach in the way these tickets are issued has become a matter of public concern. So much so that I had a regular phone-in on the radio and give after-dinner speeches on the subject.

Even Parliament got involved. As far back as 2006 I gave evidence to the Parliamentary Transport Committee, which as part of its findings, concluded that parking enforcement was 'a mess'. The Committee issued 104 recommendations, almost none of which have been implemented.

It is most gratifying to see that the more publicity is given to the poor treatment of motorists when it comes to parking tickets, the more motorists say to themselves 'We are not going to put up with this unfairness'. The end result is that motorists have begun to fight back and take on the councils.

One motorist, my dear friend Hugh Moses, did just that, and as a result his parking ticket appeal went all the way to the High Court. I am proud to say I represented Hugh at both the Parking Adjudicator and the High Court. The result, we won an amazing precedent setting victory. The effect of this far reaching High Court ruling was to demonstrate that more than £300 million of parking tickets issued in the United Kingdom were invalid and unenforceable. The full name of the case is a mouthful "London Borough of Barnet Council, R (on the application of) v The Parking Adjudicator [2006] EWHC 2357 (Admin)". Not surprisingly, it is known as "Moses – v – Barnet". The Daily Telegraph commenting on the High Court victory said "The name Hugh Moses is one which instils fear in town halls around the country. Parking managers break into a cold sweat when they hear the dreaded words "Moses v Barnet", a High Court case in which he turned the tables on councils who had ruthlessly exploited the letter of the law to raise millions of pounds in fines."

For readers who have had 'dealings' with local authorities on parking-ticket matters will know that many are amazingly arrogant when dealing with members of the public. The term 'public servant' no longer seems to apply. The fact that the system is weighted against the motorist does not help. Two examples should illustrate this:

1) Motorists must pay or appeal their parking ticket within14 days to keep an early payment discount. Thereafter they generally have 28 days from the date of service of the parking ticket to lodge an appeal. On the other hand, where formal appeals are lodged against parking tickets the council have a time limit of 56 days to respond – double the time allowed to the motorist.

2) If a motorist does not receive a document that the council claims to have sent, the onus is on the motorist to prove he or she never received it. Sometimes this even requires a witness statement to be lodged with the court. The council, on the other hand, does not have to prove they sent the document. They just have to say that they did! Fair? I leave you to be the judge.

The backlash following the Moses – v – Barnet High Court decision has given many motorists the confidence to take on the local authorities, and a prime example is the case of Ashley Finister. His was a very straightforward case. The car Ashley drives has a disabled badge because he has a child who is confined to a wheelchair and Ashley often has to rush his child to the hospital. He got eight parking tickets from his local authority because unbeknown to him his three-year blue disabled badge had expired. The council, in their infinite administrative wisdom, did not send out reminders. There was no question that he was entitled to the Blue Badge, so he wrote to the council asking for the parking tickets to be cancelled. They refused despite the fact that Mr Finister had gone to the hospital for emergency treatment for his son. Fortunately, Ashley had seen me on the TV talking about the Moses – v – Barnet High Court decision and realised that the council's parking tickets were invalid, so he lodged an appeal with the parking adjudicator.

The council treated his appeal with a certain disdain but the adjudicator agreed with Ashley and declared the council's parking tickets invalid. The council lodged a request for a review of this decision which they also lost.

The result is that all the council's parking tickets with the incorrect wording were invalid. And all because they wouldn't act fairly.

Partly because of the flood of nominees for my Crazy Parking Ticket of the Year awards, more and more stories – some funny, some sad, some just beyond belief – came to my attention. I realised it was time to publish a book which would highlight the excesses of the councils and give some comfort to readers to know that they can fight the councils and win.

The awards have taken on a life of their own. They have become internationally famous and appear on websites from Russia to Thailand. They have been featured on television, radio and in the press.

In 2005 I was approached by a brilliant and talented group of people who make viral advertisements (ads which are meant to be disseminated over the internet by a sort of virtual word-of-mouth). Together we produced three viral ads that spoofed the issue of unfair and crazy parking tickets. Two of them proved so popular that they were seen worldwide by over 5 million people and won Gold Lion Awards at the International Advertising Festival in Cannes!

The following year I commissioned another three viral ads, including one where a parking attendant paints a yellow line around a car and her colleague pops a parking ticket on the car windscreen. Astonishingly a few months later life imitated art when CCTV captured a yellow line being painted around a car and the unfortunate motorist getting a parking ticket.

So, I hope that you will enjoy the book, laugh out loud on many occasions and become outraged by the behaviour of some local authorities. Most importantly though, I hope that you will realise that you can succeed against the council if you get an unfair parking ticket and that you are not alone.

For more information visit www.appealnow.com.

Barrie Segal, 2017

A Brief History of the Parking Ticket

Since 1993 as a result of the Road Traffic Act 1991 (RTA 1991) the UK has increasingly decriminalised the issue of parking tickets, taking the matter out of the hands of the police and putting it in the hands of local authorities.

Under the RTA 1991 incorrect parking ceased to be a criminal offence but became a non-criminal 'contravention'. The new rules were first introduced by the 33 London local councils.

Subsequently more and more local councils outside London have adopted these rules so that now nearly every local authority has adopted these.

A comparison of the number of parking issued by the police under the old rules and those issued by the local councils under the new rules shows a staggering increase. Not only that, since councils took control over parking enforcement there has been an increase in the overall number of parking tickets issued in large cities.

In 1996 London Councils issued 3,246,628 parking tickets. By 2006, together with Transport for London, the number had increased to 5,075,478 and after many complaints that parking tickets were issued unfairly the 2016/2017 figure has dropped to a mere(!!) 3,539,432! Critics claim that these new rules are used just to raise money for the councils and have nothing to do the efficient movement of traffic or with road safety. I leave you to decide.

After more councils adopted decriminalised parking the number of parking tickets increased dramatically. In 2000 the total number of on street parking tickets issued in England was 4,067 of which just 636 were issued by councils outside London. By 2007 the total was 8,103 with 3,022 issued outside London

A Note on Wardens

In bringing together parking-ticket (and other motoring) stories from around the world I realised that many of the complaints received were universal – that a small minority, of parking attendants were consistently overzealous and unhelpful and are always desperate to hit their monthly targets or quotas. Of course, they have every right to be as good at their job as the rest of us but, in such positions of power, there is a line. Much has been made of this, for example, in the media recently – where it seems not a week goes past (especially in London where there are also congestion-charge issues) without a crazy parking-ticket story, or an unfair parking fine, appearing in the papers.

What is not universal, however, is the 'titles' and names of parking attendants around the world. As you'll see, it all gets rather confusing!

In the UK, for attendants employed by the police (in areas where getting a parking ticket is still a criminal offence) the correct, and official, name is Traffic Warden. In places where councils have taken over parking enforcement – and decriminalised parking-ticket enforcement – the correct, and most common, name was Parking Attendant. This was until some bright, bureaucratic spark changed it to 'Civil Enforcement Officer' in the latest parking legislation which came into force in 2008. But to add to the confusion the legislation was not adopted in Scotland where they are still called Parking Attendants.

In the USA, things are slightly different if still as confusing. Parking tickets can be issued by the police, state, county and city officials who all have different designations. Humorously, female parking attendants are often called 'Meter Maids' – a name made famous, of course, by the Beatles' song 'Lovely Rita'.

To remain consistent throughout the book, parking attendants, parking wardens, traffic wardens or even civil enforcement officers.

Crazy Parking Ticket Awards - Winners

It's our pleasure to announce the Top Ten Craziest Parking Tickets.

The votes are in the laughing – and crying – has died down.

Congratulations (or is that commiserations?) go to …

1. TRUCKING RIDICULOUS

    Truck driver Michael Collins was given a parking ticket after a burst water main had caused the road to give way and caused his 17-tonne truck to get stuck.

2. OUT ON A LIMB

    Disabled driver Peter Stapleton got a parking ticket whilst

    refitting his false leg that had fallen off whilst driving.

3. BAD NEWS COMES IN TREES

    Nicky Clegg's flattened car was given a parking ticket – after it was crushed by a tree.

4. HORSEPLAY

    Mr Robert McFarland whose horse was given a parking ticket under the heading 'Vehicle Description: brown horse'. Madness.

5. DAYLIGHT ROBBERIES

   Fred Holt was given a parking ticket whilst he was kept captive in a bank raid even though the police told the warden not to issue a ticket!

6. HOLY TICKET!

   Reverend Cletus Forson, a Brooklyn priest, received a $115 parking ticket after he rushed to hospital to administer the last rites to a dying woman.

7. HEART ATTACK

   David Holmes, while suffering severe chest pains, got a parking ticket after he drove himself to hospital.

8. NO COUNCIL SUPPORT FOR DUNDEE SUPPORTERS

   Disabled Dundee football fans' coach was given a parking ticket by the council.

9. ANOTHER FINE MESS

   A young mother was given an £80 parking ticket after she pulled over to help a choking three-month-old baby.

10. NO RESPECT

    A hearse was given a parking ticket whilst parked outside a funeral home. Need we say more?

Permit? What Permit?

When local councils start issuing parking tickets on the basis that motorists have not complied with the 'regulations' relating to the simple 'displaying' of permits, you know things are going to get heated. Some stories will make you smile. Others, however, will make you want to cry.

R-E-S-P-E-C-T

Aretha Franklin sang about R-E-S-P-E-C-T, but some parking attendants just don't have any.

Registered disabled driver Dave McSweeney was showing his respect for the dead of both World Wars by displaying a Poppy Day charity badge. However, his local council gave him a parking ticket, claiming his disabled permit was partly obscured by the poppy.

Utter poppycock.

THEY DON'T KNOW WHICH WAY IS UP

When is a blue disabled parking badge not a blue disabled parking badge? When it's not the right way up. A

Parkinson's disease sufferer John Bell, 73, got a parking ticket from Doncaster Council, supposedly after displaying his blue disabled badge upside-down.

I think it was the traffic warden who got things the wrong way round.

NOW YOU SEE IT NOW YOU DON'T

When Sally Jones had to go to a family funeral in Italy she parked her car in a disabled bay and clearly displayed her disabled permit. As she was going to be away for five days she looked carefully to make sure that there was no imminent suspension of the bay and that all was in order.

Imagine her surprise when she came back from Italy and found that she actually had three parking tickets. The first one said that she hadn't displayed her disabled permit. The second one, issued the following day, said that she had parked in a suspended bay. The third one, issued the day after, just said that she had parked illegally.

Astonishingly, when the council supplied evidence to support these parking tickets, the second parking attendant had noted in his notebook the fact that Sally's disabled permit was on display! It was only when Sally asked how they thought she had managed to magic the disabled badge into the car all the way from Italy that the council agreed to cancel the tickets.

What do I think of the traffic wardens? As Paul Daniels used to say, 'not a lot'.

A LITTLE LIGHT READING

In Martha's Vineyard, a parking judge received a somewhat silly appeal.

A married couple complained that after enjoying a romantic meal they returned to their car only to find a parking ticket neatly stuck on their car. The woman had told her husband earlier that the parking space was clearly painted with the words 'CARS ONLY'.

It was only when her husband backed the car out of the bay that he spotted that his wife had missed the first, and incidentally, most important word – 'POLICE'.

A HAT-TRICK

When highly paid footballers score a hat-trick they often get a bonus. But one motorist achieved a hat-trick he did not want – three parking tickets in 24 hours.

George Bretherton got his first ticket after forgetting to display his disabled parking badge. Fair enough. But when he returned the following day, he was absolutely determined not to get ticketed again. He carefully displayed his badge. But to his horror he then saw a parking attendant claim the badge could not be properly seen and give him another ticket.

Could things get worse? You bet. Determined to sort things out, Mr Bretherton took that parking ticket to the town hall to complain, only to find on his return that his car had been ticketed for a third time!

Mr Bretherton wrote to the council, asking them to use 'common sense' and cancel the tickets. Council? Common sense? Predictably, the council couldn't find any.

NOT FADE AWAY

The Rolling Stones once sang 'Not Fade Away', but sadly Trafford Council didn't take that message to heart.

Jane Poole, who works for Trafford Council's Children and Young People's Service, parked in a disabled bay and displayed her disabled blue badge just before midday.

However, when she returned to her car she was astonished to find that a parking ticket had been slapped on her windscreen. The reason? The section which showed who had issued the card had faded away.

When Jane rang up to complain, she was told that there was a problem with the stamping ink used on all the Trafford Blue badges that expired between January and June 2007 – it faded in the sun and was no longer legible. So, what about her parking ticket? Jane was told it couldn't be annulled and she would have to appeal.

And to resolve the faded badge problem? Disabled drivers were told to post their badge back to the council for a new one, or make a potentially difficult journey to the council's office – each leaving the now non-permitted car ripe for another parking ticket.

If only parking tickets were written in the same magical stamping ink ...

WAR VETERAN COMES OUT FIGHTING!

Ex-RAF war veteran Bob Thackray (78) and his partner Mrs Lucy Rawsthorne (79) went shopping in Colne town centre and, as usual, displayed their disabled badge. They were therefore astonished to find on their return that a parking warden had struck and slapped a parking ticket on their car allegedly for not showing the badge's expiry date correctly.

The couple contested the fine, saying that the warden could easily have seen the expiry date if he had looked more closely. But were told that they were in the wrong

... because a windscreen wiper was blocking the badge's expiry date.

It makes fighting for your country so worthwhile, doesn't it? DYK

WHAT IS A 10p PARKING TICKET WORTH?

What would you do if a council claimed that you did not display a 10p parking ticket and slapped you with a £30 fine? Well, it happened to former marine Nick Newby and he decided to fight it.

Mr Newby wrote to the Kirklees Council saying he couldn't see the car park's pay-and-display signs. He also suggested that they should cancel the charge on the grounds of common sense. The council refused his request. As a matter of principle Mr Newby refused to pay the £30 fine.

The council then took Mr Newby to court where after several court appearances he was fined £50 and ordered to pay £250 towards the council's costs incurred. Mr Newby appealed against the conviction to the High Court in Leeds. At the hearing the council's barrister told Judge Rodney Grant that the car park in question was now free. The Judge commented, "I am speechless." Astonishingly, legal argument continued for a full day and the case was adjourned to be heard at a later date.

According to the Huddersfield Daily Examiner Mr Newby's fine was upheld at Leeds Crown Court he was given an absolute discharge. As a result, the paper reports that the council was left with legal costs of between £5,000 and £10,000.

TRUCKING RIDICULOUS – OUTRIGHT WINNER!!

It was a normal day for truck driver Michael Collins, who was on his way to collect a skip in London's Belsize Park. But then, without warning, his truck lurched as the ground beneath him collapsed. Unbeknown to Michael, a burst water main had caused the road to give way, creating a deep hole where the front wheels of his 17-tonne struck became stuck.

While he was waiting for his truck to be rescued a passing parking attendant appeared. To the astonishment of nearby residents and despite Michael's protests she stood on tiptoe and whacked a parking ticket on the truck's windscreen, uttering the immortal words, 'You can appeal'.

The truck was owned by family firm Meyers, whose director Kenneth Meyer said: 'We've had a few questionable parking tickets but this one takes the biscuit.' Initially, Camden Council said that the firm should appeal. But after clearly realising the absurdity of the situation a red-faced Camden Council press official said the ticket would be cancelled. The council said that they would be apologising to the driver and talking to the parking attendant.

Memo to Camden Council: If you have dug yourself a deep hole ... know when to stop digging!

THE MOST EXPENSIVE PARKING TICKET IN THE WORLD?

Here's a story that might make you think twice about giving someone a lift, and appealing when you get fined for doing so. In February 2005, Ryan Williams dropped a passenger off in Cowbridge, South Wales, near a pedestrian crossing. A policeman saw him pull up, and reported him for illegally parking on the zig-zag lines. Ryan Williams, however, denied parking on the zig-zag lines, and decided to appeal.

Appeal he did. Over the next eighteen months, Ryan Williams appeared before Barry Magistrates thirteen times. For various reasons the hearings were adjourned, because of missing witnesses, unavailable courtrooms for a full hearing and insufficient time to hear the case amongst others. Mr Williams eventually gave up when one of his witnesses failed to testify. After his defeat, Mr Williams, a clerical officer, said: 'People might think I'm mad but I don't regret it. I was determined to try to prove my innocence however much it cost.'

Ah yes. The cost. As well as the £60 fine and £150 prosecution costs, Ryan will have to find £7,500 in defence fees to his solicitor. Observers estimate that court and police administrative and legal costs have cost the taxpayer £35,000. If the time taken to drop his passenger was five seconds then the total costs come to more than

£8,000 per second, or a mere £30 million per hour.

Suddenly, those multi-storey fees don't seem so expensive ...

A PENNY FOR YOUR THOUGHTS

This story all started when Emma Dawes didn't have any coins for the parking meter in the Old Market car park in Dartford. Leaving her three-year-old son in the car, she nipped to a nearby shop to get some change. But when she returned, fifty pence permit in hand, she found a £30 ticket on the windscreen. Despite protests, the parking attendant wouldn't cancel the ticket. Dartford Council too, were equally unresponsive, and insisted the fine be paid.

So, Emma and her husband Adam did pay the fine, but in their own unique way. The couple turned up to Dartford Civic Centre with the £30 ... all in one and two pence pieces. Unable to weigh the bag, the cashier had to count out the coins by hand – all while Emma and Adam read the papers nearby. It took the cashier a very satisfying forty five minutes to count.

That's what I call change for good.

DID YOU KNOW?
THE PARKING METER

Although it is sometimes disputed, Carl C. Magee, of Oklahoma City, Oklahoma, is generally credited with inventing the parking meter. The world's first parking meter installed was in Oklahoma City, on July 16, 1935. The world, in unison, heaved a heavy sigh.

The first parking meters introduced in the UK were in 1958 and were operated by clockwork and needed winding up with a large key!

London's first parking meter went up in Grosvenor Square, Mayfair. Parking has remained extortionate there ever since! Initially, 625 parking meters were installed around the country and it cost the modern equivalent of 2p an hour to park with a fixed penalty of £2.

Today the fine can cost as high as £130, with a discount of £65 for prompt payment. How times have changed!

Don't Park with Animals or Children

Never work with animals or children, the old Hollywood saying goes. Well, the same applies for travelling as most stressed parents will tell you. Throw insufferable parking ticket attendants into the mix ... and you've got yourself an explosive cocktail of incompetence, stress and a stupid disregard for intelligence.

A LOAD OF BULLOCKS

What's the difference between a dead cow and a car? Not much, according to the parking authorities in Rutherford County, Tennessee, who presumably having decided that irate drivers were more trouble than they were worth, found a new way of fulfilling their quota by targeting deceased animals instead.

The two cows in question belonged to a farmer in Murfreesboro. Sadly, he had to have them put down, and had left the bodies by his house, which backs onto the road, for collection. But when the waste disposal company failed to pick up the dead livestock, the parking authorities moved in. Describing the cows as 'unattended vehicles', they issued each with a ticket.

When the farmer complained, the local sheriff department's response was that they thought the cows were asleep.

IT MAKES YOU SICK

A mother who took her sick child out of her car and put him in a stroller to buy a Pay and Display voucher received a parking ticket before she got back to her car with the voucher. When she appealed to Barnet Council they wrote back and said she had taken too long buy the voucher and should have locked her child in the car to save time!

The council subsequently apologised for their heartless response.

HORSE PLAY!

You leave your horse in the street and what do you expect to find when you get back? Some doodoo possibly but not a parking ticket.

Retired blacksmith Robert McFarland was flabbergasted to find a parking ticket slapped on his horse Charlie Boy. Mr McFarland, a tour guide in the Yorkshire Dales, spotted that under the heading 'vehicle description' the cheeky warden had written 'brown horse'.

The council eventually apologised and cancelled the ticket. Charlie Boy's comment on the council was somewhat less printable.

THE LAW IS AN ASS

Animal lover Louise Whyte took her 17-year-old pet donkey Aimée to Worthing to raise funds for the Sussex Horse Rescue Trust. When she finished her collection three hours later she returned to Aimée's horsebox – only to find a £30 parking ticket on it.

An astonished Louise said 'I couldn't believe it. I had a permit in the windscreen and thought the wardens would show a bit of initiative.'

Mrs Whyte said that she planned to appeal and take her donkey with her if summoned to court. Whether the one who wrote out the ticket would be attending too is unclear.

MY BUNNY RABBIT GOT A PARKING TICKET

It started off like any other day for pet-shop owner Cliff Chamberlain. He had been parked for 15 minutes outside his pet shop in Eccles, Greater Manchester unloading sand from his truck. He had left his rabbit 'Bugsy' in its hutch in the van when he spotted a parking attendant photographing him. Although he was legally parked when he was unloading, Mr Chamberlain decided to take no chances, popped Bugsy's hutch on the ground and drove his truck to a car park next door before any parking ticket could be issued. You would think.

In Cliff's absence, the parking attendant issued the parking ticket and tried to give it to Cliff when he returned. Cliff naturally refused to accept it. The parking attendant, clearly persistent in her goal, then tried to fob it off onto a young man who had turned up for a job interview. When he too refused the attendant said 'Well, someone's got to have it!' and promptly stuck it on poor Bugsy's hutch – a breach of the Road Traffic Act.

'I'm fed up,' said Cliff after the astounding incident, 'and so is the rabbit – his hutch hasn't even got wheels.'

Eventually the council cancelled the ticket. Bugsy was unavailable for comment though a few weeks later gave birth to six healthy bunnies.

(Mr Chamberlain and Bugsy were the first winners of appealnow.com's Crazy Parking Tickets Awards.)

THE TICKETS ARRIVED TWO BY TWO …

Here's a story on the verge of insanity.

When visitors arrived to spend a day out at Blackpool Zoo, parking problems led to staff directing drivers to park on a nearby grass verge. But a fun family trip turned sour when the visitors returned to their vehicles to find Traffic Wardens had also been enjoying a great day out in their own unique way. Every single car had a parking ticket.

The Zoo initially agreed to pay the £1500 fine on behalf of the drivers, until an embarrassed Blackpool Council agreed to write off the tickets.

STRICTLY FOR THE BIRDS

After receiving an emergency call about an injured bird that was lying in the street an RSPCA inspector dashed to the rescue.

Having parked his car next to the pavement to attend to the injured bird, the caring animal helper was surprised to be given a parking ticket for his efforts. As it turns out this was not the first occasion that an RSPCA inspector had received a parking ticket whilst tending to an injured animal.

'The Council is investigating,' a spokesperson claimed. Yes, we've heard that one before!

A WHALE OF A TIME

You may remember this story – it united the country, generated world-wide interest and touched the hearts of the British people.

Whilst brave divers were trying to rescue the 18ft baby whale that had lost its way in the Thames in 2006, and was close to becoming beached in the Thames shallow waters, Transport for London and Wandsworth Council tried to pull a fast one ... and gave the divers' vehicles parking tickets while they were in the water! What's even more remarkable is that police had earlier given the divers special permission to park!

And we thought the whale was confused!

> **DID YOU KNOW?**
>
> From 1st April 2015 CCTV cameras were banned from being used for parking enforcement in England except for use where vehicles have parked on a "Keep Clear" zig-zag outside schools, in Bus lanes, on Red Routes and in Bus stops.
>
> CCTV also continues to be used for moving traffic contraventions, e.g. turning right where a sign prohibits it and for enforcing travelling in a bus lane and yellow box junctions.

Crash-Bang-Wallop what a Ticket!

Car crashes are horrific – no matter how small or how few people are involved. Now imagine, a parking-ticket attendant coming along ... it's madness, I tell you!

ADDING INSULT TO INJURY

Just when Sue Hamer thought nothing else could go wrong, it did.

Sue's car had just been written off in a rush-hour collision in Altringham and on top of that she was hurt and had to be taken to hospital. Could things get worse? Well, yes, because whilst she was being treated for her injuries her smashed car was given a parking ticket by a passing parking attendant.

Sounds like someone needs a crash course in common sense.

YES, IT CAN GET WORSE!

Craig Gillon didn't think it could get worse after his Peugeot car was hit by a suspected joyrider. Not only was there body damage, but the car couldn't be driven. Then to cap it all an over-zealous parking attendant gave the smashed car a parking ticket!

Onlookers told the parking attendant how they had heard a bang as the suspected joyriders smashed into Craig's car. However, the Lambeth parking attendant was unmoved and ticketed the smashed-up vehicle. One eyewitness said that the car had been hit by a Vauxhall Corsa, whose driver had raced away and then abandoned the car up the road.

A bystander said he had spoken to the attendant and told her that there had been an accident and the car had been pushed up the path. The attendant replied that the car owner could appeal.

If only the attendant had a better nature that could be appealed to.

IMMOVABLE CAR, IMMOVABLE WARDEN

Another wrecked car. Another sensitive traffic warden.

That was the experience of the owner of a wrecked VW Golf in Barkingside, Essex who was shocked when he arrived at his car to find that a parking attendant had whacked a £100 parking fine on the car shortly after the accident.

A passer-by took photos of the incident and told the warden that what he was doing was atrocious but the parking attendant told him to go away and that it was illegal to take pictures. Astonishingly the next day the wrecked car, which could not be driven, was given yet another ticket by the very same warden.

Warms the heart, doesn't it?

THEM'S THE BRAKES!

If your brake lights aren't working, you're a hazard to other motorists. So, when another motorist warned Roy Deacon that his were faulty, he immediately pulled over to repair them.

So far, so responsible driving. But while Roy was reading his handbook to find out where to fit a replacement fuse, he was shocked to see a traffic warden write out a ticket and place it on his windscreen.

Roy, a driving instructor from South West London, said afterwards: 'I would have been breaking the law if I had driven knowing both brake lights were out. All the warden had to do was ask me what I was doing but he just put the ticket on the window and walked off.'

If only traffic wardens knew when to stop.

ALL FIRED UP

It's a bad day when your car is stolen. It doesn't get any better when the thieves leave it as a burnt-out wreck. But at least you can rely on traffic wardens not to exacerbate the situation further.

If only that last part was true. For when wardens saw the burnt-out wreck of a stolen vehicle in Edinburgh, they were unable to 'steal' themselves and walk away.

Despite the car having no tyres, no windows, or even a windscreen on which to place the tickets, three tickets were issued in quick succession.

> DID YOU KNOW?
>
> According to the magazine Auto Express, Britain's most expensive parking space was sold back in 2014 for an astonishing £400,000. The garage in Kensington, West London is underground and has space for three cars.

BUS STOP? JUST STOP!

To Highgate, North London, where Neil Rutter experienced one of those dreadful motoring moments – the car battery dying on you and the car's electrical system shutting down. As his car's power steering failed, Neil managed to pull over and leave his car at the side of the road. It was parked legally, and Neil even left a note on the dashboard, explaining that the car was broken down, and he was going to arrange for someone to repair it.

That should have been that. But then, before a breakdown vehicle could be arranged, a group of workmen turned up, unannounced, to paint a new bus stop where Neil's car had broken down. Not that a car was going to stop them doing their work – they simply painted the new bus stop around it. And then, before the paint was even dry, a friendly neighbourhood warden was on hand to ticket the broken-down car.

Neil Rutter told the Hornsey Journal, 'Anyone with a bit of sense would have seen that the car's broken down.'

A traffic warden? No sense? Never heard of that before …

> DID YOU KNOW?
>
> WESTMINSTER WORST TOP TEN
>
> Westminster City Council is owed more than a million pounds in parking fines, £1,216,905 to be exact!
>
> The worst offenders are vehicles from France (£356,000 – 29.6%), Qatar (£191,105 – 15.7%), the UAE (£116,030 – 9.5%) and Romania (£114,235 – 9.4%)
>
> The council has announced that it is in the early stages of testing a process of obtaining a judgment in the UK against foreign persistent evaders, with the potential to transfer proceedings abroad.

Star Parking

Celebrities all over the world are forever using their name, fame and wealth to wriggle out of things. Well, thankfully for us, for some celebrities the Star Card is not universally accepted.

DO YOU HAVE THE TIME? YES

Radio broadcasters are used to working to split-second timings, but the timing of one parking attendant baffled even BBC London presenter and actress JoAnne Good.

JoAnne returned one minute late to a parking bay. Her pay and display voucher expired at 3.40 p.m., and the time shown on the meter was 3.41. She approached a parking attendant who confirmed that the council gave five minutes' grace before issuing a parking ticket. JoAnne breathed a sigh of relief, but to her astonishment the parking attendant said his watch showed 3.45 and promptly slapped a parking ticket on her car.

JoAnne says she insisted that the parking attendant take a photograph of the time on the meter and his watch but he refused.

THAT'S NOT LIFE

Esther Rantzen is famous for sorting out people's problems on her popular BBC programme That's Life, but there was one problem even she couldn't sort out.

It all started when Esther had just 10 minutes to get to an important lunch. She had parked her car in Grosvenor Square in London when she discovered the pay-and-display machine wouldn't accept her coins. Fortunately (if that is the word) she spotted a passing parking attendant. The parking attendant told her to get a ticket from another pay-and-display machine on the other side of the square. She did this but when she returned to her car with her ticket in her hand, guess what? That's right – her car had already been ticketed.

Esther Rantzen said afterwards, 'I have done stories on That's Life about people in all kinds of situations getting parking tickets but I thought those days had long gone.'

If only. Esther's appeal to Westminster Council was turned down, on the grounds that the machines were not out of order. But after the story was highlighted in the press, the ticket was eventually cancelled.

ONE LAW FOR US ...

Good looking. Hugely successful. Dates some of the most glamorous women in the world ... If all that wasn't enough, Jude Law has yet another string to his bow that we mortals can only dream about – getting off parking tickets.

When heartthrob Jude Law went shopping in Notting Hill, he received the usual admiring glances from passers-by ... with one exception: the parking attendant, who was less interested in the star, and more in where his car was parked.

The attendant was about to issue a ticket to the Hollywood star when the actor spotted him. He dashed out of the shop to speak to the attendant. Remarkably the film heartthrob managed to persuade the parking attendant not to issue a parking ticket. According to one passer-by, Law, the star of Closer, The Aviator, All the King's Men, and Breaking and Entering, argued that the warden was only issuing the ticket to 'get his face in the papers'.

So, while many of us may plead with attendants to let us off tickets, the star of The Talented Mr Ripley proved that a silver screen tongue really can make a difference.

NOT SO LUCKY STAR

Not all stars are as fortunate as Jude Law. When megastar Madonna went for her gym workout local parking attendants also limbered up – to issue parking tickets.

After Madonna arrived in her chauffeur-driven car and went for her workout, nearby parking attendants exercised by slapping £100 parking fines on the car while her driver waited on a yellow line.

Newspaper sources reported that parking attendants issued her cars with more than 50 tickets, totalling at least £2,500 in fines.

Witnesses said Madonna's driver attempted to avoid the tickets by continually driving the car backwards and forwards – after all, you can't get a parking ticket if you're not actually parked. But the parking attendants ticketed him anyway. Who knows – maybe they'd heard Madonna's version of 'American Pie'.

TICKET ME BABY ONE MORE TIME

Britney Spears is renowned for causing controversy and trouble. If she's not shaving her hair off, she's baring her midriff, or snogging Madonna.

But the mother-of-two and 'Toxic' singer also seems to disobey parking laws. On leaving a spa in Bel-Air, not only was she surrounded by adoring fans and paparazzi but also a parking-ticket attendant who was busy slapping a fine on her car ... for all to see.

Oops, she's done it again.

RED CARD FOR UNITED STAR

Rio Ferdinand is one of the most famous soccer players in the UK. Yet even he is not immune from parking tickets.

Mr Ferdinand's £160,000 Aston Martin Vanquish got ticketed for parking outside an official bay in Manchester's King Street. The parking attendant ticketed the car because it would not fit into the official bay.

An unusual case, then, of a footballer being hauled up for not putting the boot in.

BILL FOR THE BILL STAR

Actor Gary Whelan is well known as Inspector Harry Haines in ITV's famous police show The Bill. However, he found himself on the other side of the law when he stopped outside his bank in Brighton.

Unable to find a space nearby, Gary stopped outside the branch while he nipped (nicked?) in. But it didn't take long before he was rushing out again, as another customer told him he was being issued with a ticket.

Gary, who drives a Bentley, attempted to defuse the situation with a joke, asking the warden 'How can I afford to pay that?' But the local constabulary who appeared were anything but laughing policemen – Gary was issued with a stop and search ticket, for being 'abusive to parking attendant'.

Gary had the last laugh though. He auctioned the ticket for the children's charity Whoopsadaisy.

> **DID YOU KNOW?**
>
> **PARKING LEGISLATION**
>
> The Traffic Management Act 2004 applies to both England and Wales.
>
> There are 22 additional pieces of legislation which apply to parking and moving traffic enforcement.
>
> Scotland did not adopt The Traffic Management Act 2004 and continues parking enforcement under the Road Traffic Act 1991.
>
> The above legislation does not include legislation relating to
>
> Bus Lane enforcement in England and Wales.
>
> Congestion Charging in London
>
> Dartford River Crossing legislation
>
> Mersey Gateway Bridge Crossings legislation
>
> Durham Congestion Charge legislation

THE PEN IS MIGHTIER THAN THE PENCIL

When is a parking permit not a parking permit? When it's filled out in pencil.

BBC newsreader Anna Ford has read out many stories over the years, but none can be as bizarre as the ticket given to the builder fixing her roof. Ford had given the builder a visitor's permit to park while he worked, but because he hadn't filled it out in pen, the traffic warden ruled it invalid, and ticketed his vehicle.

Ford attempted twice to have the ticket overturned to no avail. Hounslow Council's response was 'There are clear printed instructions on the back of the visitor permit asking that the entry is completed in ink, to prevent fraud, as pencilled information can be erased.'

KATE MIDDLETON GETS A PARKING TICKET

We all know that miserable feeling when you go to your car and see the parking attendant writing a parking ticket. What's worse, he hands it to you there and then. Well it happens to everyone – including the girl we all expected to be a future Queen of England.

Kate Middleton, the Duchess of Cambridge, had that same experience when she was given a parking ticket for her VW Golf when she left her old Chelsea home. Although she had a resident's permit she didn't spot that the Council had suspended the residents' bay in which she had parked.

A spokesman for the contractors that issue tickets on the council's behalf said, 'It is a tribute to her that she handled the incident in precisely the way one would expect of a future Queen.'

DID YOU KNOW?
THE HIGHEST PARKING REVENUES IN LONDON

According to the Sun newspaper the 10 London councils with the highest parking revenues are:

Westminster: £76.4m

Kensington & Chelsea: £46.1m

Camden: £38.1m

Hammersmith & Fulham: £35.6m

Wandsworth: £30.4m

Islington: £29.7m

Lambeth: £27.5m

Haringey: £25.4m

Hackney: £23.3m

Ealing: £21.4m

It's Not Just Cars

It's upsetting to find a parking ticket on your car. Whether you are a senior policeman or an RAC motor mechanic. But a doctor 'on call'? Proof that nobody is safe from a parking ticket attack.

BLOODY RIDICULOUS

'Do Something Amazing Today' runs the slogan of the National Blood Service. In Sutton, a traffic warden did just that, though not along the lines of 'Save a life. Give Blood' that the advert intended.

For four years, a mobile National Blood Service truck has visited Sutton, parking at the same spot outside a group of offices, so volunteers can give blood. But seeing the good citizens of the town turn up and exchange a pint of the red stuff in return for a cup of tea and a biscuit was too much of a temptation for one parking attendant. Whilst those inside were giving blood, the parking attendant gave in his own unique way – in the form of a parking ticket.

Sutton council eventually waived the fine, saying the parking attendant had made a simple error of judgment. Or to put it more aptly, a rush of blood to the head.

SKIP THE PARKING TICKETS

Are you a builder? Do you keep getting parking tickets when you work? Well, one builder who got fed up with receiving parking tickets outside the property he was renovating came up with a novel idea on how to stop getting them.

He paid the local council for a skip licence and hired a skip with a dropdown front and parked it in front of the property. Every day when he arrived for work, he let down the drop down front, drove his van into the skip and pulled up the front!

He has not received a parking ticket since, much to the chagrin of the local parking attendant.

ASSAULT AND BATTERY

There are some vehicles you might consider to be immune from getting a parking ticket – ambulances for example.

But that's not so, as driver Darren Broughton discovered, when he stopped his ambulance to buy some batteries for the defibrillator equipment. A warden, clearly suffering from a bad case of yellow-line fever, was unable to stop himself from ticketing the vehicle.

Unfortunately, Darren's ambulance did not have a machine to detect whether the warden had a heart.

IT WAS KISMET ... OR WAS THAT SEKHMET?

A Liverpool crane driver, Billy Brindle, almost got a parking ticket whilst moving a 3,500-year-old stone statue of the lion-headed goddess of war Sekhmet into the Liverpool Museum's new building.

The whole operation had to be stopped whilst the crane driver tried to persuade a parking attendant not to issue a parking ticket. The Council said the parking attendant was just doing his job, that no ticket was issued and that it was just 'a breakdown in communication'.

The pig-headed God of War-dens, Tikhet, was unavailable for comment.

STAMP IT OUT, GUYS

'The mail must get through' was the motto of the famous Pony Express. So too for the Royal Mail. But the Wild West came to London some years ago when Royal Mail vans were ambushed by savage parking attendants.

Royal Mail van drivers picking up mail for delivery at the Post Office sorting office in Victoria were surrounded by parking attendants who had been hiding ready to attack at precisely 8.30 am to give each van a parking ticket as they waited to load the mailbags.

A FAIR COP?

None of us is immune when it comes to parking tickets.

Former top cop Sir Paul Stephenson also picked up a parking fine when he was Deputy Commissioner of the Metropolitan Police. The irony is that it happened while he was talking to callers on the BBC's Drive Time radio show.

Commissioner Stephenson's Range Rover was ticketed because the driver had forgotten to display the exemption disk police are allowed to use when on official business.

I don't know if Commissioner Stephenson suffers from back pain, but certainly he knows the pain of a slipped disc.

NO RESPECT

The solemnity of a funeral was marred when a passing parking attendant whacked a parking ticket on the waiting hearse. The hearse was parked on double yellow lines outside funeral directors McKenzie & Millar when it got the £60 fine. Outraged directors at the firm said that they would fight the ticket.

In an amazing statement Edinburgh City Council claimed the ticket was correct because the coffin was not yet in the hearse! They also said that the parking attendant could not see any staff from the undertaker's!

McKenzie & Millar, said that while preparations were being made to load the coffin into the hearse, the vehicle was left unattended for about five minutes. The spokesman told the BBC, 'We have nowhere else to park. To park the vehicle elsewhere would mean we'd have to walk down the street holding a coffin, which would be inappropriate.'

There's something else I can think of that's inappropriate, too.

(Legal Note: Any vehicle, including a hearse, can stop to load heavy goods or parcels on a single or double yellow line if there are no loading restrictions posted – a hearse waiting for a coffin to be loaded would come under this general exemption even if there was no specific exemption for funerals.)

A NASTY TACKLE

The Scotland rugby team had trained hard for their international match against Romania and thought that they were well prepared for their match. They were however unprepared for one particular pre-match event when the Scotland rugby team bus received a ticket shortly before the game.

Not exactly getting behind your team is it? What a piece of scrum.

WHAT DO YOU WANT ... BLOOD?

Some things just make your blood boil ...

The Blood Transfusion Service had received permission to park their bus in Cockburn Street, Edinburgh. But their bus had to stop on a yellow line because two cars were illegally parked in its designated bay. As the good people of Edinburgh donated happily away, the 'Enforcers' showed their own blood group was a negative one with a £60 fine.

The blood donors should have had tea and biscuits as a reward, but in this case the parking attendant took the biscuit.

DID YOU KNOW?
MAKING HISTORY

The first ever High Court decision on the validity of a parking ticket was made on 2nd August 2006. The landmark decision was a victory for motorist Hugh Moses, who not only challenged the correctness of their claimed issue but also challenged the validity of two parking tickets issued by Barnet Council. The High Court found that on the evidence that neither parking ticket was correctly issued but more importantly that the tickets were invalid and legally unenforceable as they did not have two dates; both the date of the contravention and the date of issue.

The case R (London Borough of Barnet) -v- The Parking and Traffic Appeals Service means that some 6.4 million parking tickets issued each year in the UK were invalid.

Following the judgement hundreds of councils rapidly changed the wording of their parking tickets but amazingly many did not and continued issuing illegal parking tickets.

A RIGHT FIX

RAC mechanic John Gallacher got a reward for fixing a motorist's broken-down car – a parking ticket.

Mr Gallacher had only left his RAC van for five minutes to drive the silver Peugeot he had been working on around the block to check that the steering was fixed. In the brief time he was gone a passing 'Enforcer' popped a £30 parking ticket on his windscreen. Not unreasonably, Mr Gallacher said he thought the flashing orange lights on the roof of his van would have made it clear that he was parked in a residents-only zone attending an emergency.

Perhaps the parking attendant thought that the flashing emergency lights belonged to a mobile disco.

BUS(TED)

Picture the situation. You're a bus driver. You're driving your bus. You see a queue of people waiting for you at a bus stop. You pull over into the bus stop, and – as the name suggests – stop your bus to the let passengers on. So far, so good. But wait, not everyone wants to buy a ticket. This chap in the queue wants to give you one instead…

This was the extraordinary scene that greeted Manchester bus driver Chris O'Mahony, when he stopped his number 77 bus to let people on. He and his passengers looked on in absolute disbelief as the Manchester City Council parking attendant joined the queue to prepare the parking ticket, deposited the £40 notice and then walked away. The bus driver's crime? Parking in a restricted area.

Chris told the Manchester Evening News: 'I asked "Restricted to who?"' He said, "Buses". Then he said I shouldn't be parking there – but passengers were still getting on. I said to him twice "I'm at a bus stop" but that didn't make a difference. The attendant said he'd been told to issue tickets to buses that park.'

Manchester City Council bosses cancelled the ticket and ordered the warden to be retrained.

> DID YOU KNOW?
>
> The first United Kingdom local authority to issue more than 1 million parking tickets was Westminster Council in 2004. The council issued a mind-blowing 1,051,798 parking tickets, an increase of 7.7% from the previous year when they issued 976,476 tickets.

One Good Deed Deserves a Ticket

KARMA

Karma is a simple concept. Most people live their life by it – you do a good deed and life rewards you back. As far as some traffic wardens are concerned, however, karma is just something to slap a ticket on.

NO FARE – UNFAIR

When a London taxi driver went to jump-start the car of a seriously ill woman little did he think he would end up with a parking ticket for his good deed.

Holloway taxi driver Joe Cartwright went to help motorist Linda Dingley, who needed to collect medication that had been left at a relative's house, but found her car battery was flat. So, Mr Cartwright double-parked his taxi alongside her car to be close enough to connect jump-leads to start her car. But, in the mere moments it took to collect the leads from Mrs Dingley's house, he returned to find a parking ticket on his cab!

Mr Cartwright's appeal to Islington Council was rejected, the council claiming lack of evidence. Personally, I think the council was lacking in something else.

THE MAIL MUST GET THROUGH

What do you do when you see a postman struggling with a heavy sack of mail? If you're nice person, you might offer to give him a hand. And if you're a traffic warden ...

The postman in question was parked on a single yellow line with parking-time restrictions. He left a note on the dashboard stating that he was delivering to the next road. The traffic warden in question sat on his moped and watched him wobble around the corner with the heavy sack. When the postman returned, he saw the traffic warden had posted something of his own on his vehicle ... a ticket. And, surprise, surprise, as the postman approached him, he quickly drove away.

All part and parcel of a traffic warden's day.

NO GOOD DEED GOES UNPUNISHED – PART ONE (WITH ACKNOWLEDGEMENTS TO CRISTOPHER EVENS)

When taxi driver Misar Ahmed stopped to phone for an ambulance for a passenger who had been taken ill while in his taxi he was shocked to receive a parking ticket ... whilst he was on the phone!

To make matters worse the council, astonishingly, would not cancel the parking ticket, but insisted that he should lodge a formal appeal!

NO GOOD DEED GOES UNPUNISHED – PART TWO

It gets worse!

Having received an urgent call from a panicked local parishioner, Reverend Cletus Forson, a Brooklyn priest, rushed to the local hospital to administer the last rites to a dying patient. Absolutely desperate to find a priest for her daughter's last remaining hours, the patient's elderly mother called the Reverend – in bed with the flu at the time – and asked for his help. The priest was even told there was 'no time to spare'.

On arrival, there were no available parking spaces but the reverend was compelled to help. 'It is my obligation to get there and minister to the needs of the sick,' the priest claimed in court, having just sworn an oath on the Bible.

Rev. Forson had placed his official 'Clergy On Call' parking permit on the dashboard and was inside the hospital for less than twenty minutes. For all of his heavenly assistance, Mr Forson was issued with a $115 parking fine. The Reverend appealed against the ticket in court but Judge Michael Ciaravino threw out the claim citing that 'attending to a patient at a hospital is not a valid defence to the violation'. Ciaravino's guilty verdict was final.

Reverend Forson's church ended up paying the fine.

NO GOOD DEED GOES UNPUNISHED – PART THREE

It seems no matter what you do – even if you are obeying one of the ten commandments – there's always a traffic warden just around the corner waiting to pounce. In a case of love thy neighbour, a good Samaritan couple got more than they bargained for when rushing their neighbour and friend, who was in the midst of having a major seizure, to the local surgery for emergency treatment.

Fred Welsh and wife Patricia were furious after two Police Community Support Officers (PCSOs) issued a £30 parking ticket while Mrs Welsh was inside the Easington surgery doing her bit for neighbourhood watch. Astonishingly, during the four minutes that Patricia was away from her vehicle, two PCSOs showed no mercy and issued a ticket. On her arrival back at the car, Mrs Welsh tried to explain what had happened but the wardens wouldn't listen. Mr Walsh said, 'I'm absolutely fuming. We were just trying to do a neighbour a good turn. Where is the community spirit?'

A Durham Constabulary spokesman later commented, 'We have a tried and tested procedure for dealing with disputed fixed-penalty tickets. The couple involved have twenty eight days in which to appeal against it.'

HEART OF STONE

An astonished Age Concern volunteer was given a parking ticket as she stopped to help three elderly people get out of her car.

Initially Poole Council turned down her appeal but after a local newspaper made enquiries, the council did a U-turn and cancelled the ticket. (This was no great act of charity by the council as the parking ticket should never have been issued in the first place – see legal note below.)

George Hattemore, chairman of Broadstone Age Concern Day Centre, who was faced with having to cancel the old folks' next outing to pay the fine said, 'It shows you that sometimes a bit of pressure in the right place does help. We did really feel they were being extremely unreasonable.'

The incident arose when volunteer driver Christine Webb took three elderly ladies to Branksome Dene at the end of August, where the day centre had booked the community room for a day out.

She parked close to the entrance and helped the women – in their late 80s and 90s – into the building.

When she returned to buy a pay-and-display ticket a parking warden had issued one of his own.

(Legal Note: The law allows you to stop on a single or double yellow line to let passengers get out. It also allows the driver to assist them if they are elderly, young or cannot walk well, WITHOUT having to pay for parking. The council should have cancelled the ticket immediately that they were aware of the position.)

SUNDAY BLIGHT AT THE LONDON PALLADIUM

It was a very enjoyable day for Margaret Carter because her granddaughter was appearing at the London Palladium.

Because Margaret had difficulty walking and getting about, her neighbour Christopher Smith had kindly driven her to the London Palladium, parked his car legally and they had both gone off to see the show.

Margaret couldn't walk very far, so after the show Christopher went to collect his car, stopped outside the Palladium and walked over to escort Margaret to the car, a matter of two minutes.

To their surprise, when they got back to the car they saw a car clamper starting to clamp the car. Christopher asked the clamper not to do this as he had an elderly passenger and they had a long distance to travel. Christopher even volunteered to pay the clamping charge providing the car wasn't clamped. The clamper told him to 'bugger off' and proceeded to clamp the car.

As a result, Margaret and Christopher had to wait an hour and a half for the car to be unclamped before they could set off on their long journey home. An appeal was lodged against the clamping ticket, and in record time the council cancelled the ticket and refunded the money, but without one single word of apology.

A CHRISTMAS PRESENT FOR SANTA – A PARKING TICKET

The sick children at Birmingham Children's Hospital were looking forward to Santa's annual visit. Ray Hickinbotham, chairman of the Young at Heart children's charity was having a great time dressed as Santa and handing out beautiful presents to the hospital's poorly children.

To get to the hospital, Mr Hickinbotham had parked the charity's minibus in a taxi rank outside because police cars had filled the street. Unbeknown to our Santa – he was dishing out the pressies to sick children remember – his charity's minibus was getting an unwanted present from the local council – a parking ticket.

Tra la la la la …

A FINE CHRISTMAS

Some residents with unpaid parking tickets in the Canadian province of Alberta got a very welcome Christmas gift.

Canadian parking authority Impark teamed up with the Salvation Army for one day last year so that if you brought the Sally Ann a new 'unwrapped' toy to help out a child for Christmas, you got your parking ticket waived.

There was an added bonus – it didn't matter if you had one unpaid ticket or ten, because for each toy you brought, a ticked was cancelled. A good swap indeed and a clever little scheme.

CHRISTMAS DISPIRITED

Vince Donnan looked resplendent in his Father Christmas costume as he was collecting money for children in a local hospital. Unfortunately, the Land Rover towing his sled broke down on double yellow lines in High Wycombe.

A passing traffic warden spotted the vehicle, called for 'advice' from his supervisor and then promptly wrote out a parking ticket. Driver of the Land Rover – the reindeer if you will – Rod Barber was utterly flabbergasted. 'I'm collecting money for a children's ward of the local hospital,' Mr Barber told the warden, pleading not to ticket Santa's modern sleigh.

'I'm only doing my job,' said the warden as Santa looked on dismayed

Guess whose going on the 'naughty' list?

CHRISTMAS BONUS

Getting a parking ticket around Christmas time is not the sort of present you want. But a parking-ticket Santa brightened up many motorists' day.

In 2006, last-minute shoppers in Birmingham were delighted to find their vehicles had been given £30 neatly tucked under their parking tickets together with a card.

The card read: 'Don't let this ticket spoil your Christmas – here's £30 to pay it off.'

It was signed, 'Merry Christmas, parking ticket Santa.' If only the Easter Bunny did the same!

GOOD SAMARITAN

Samaritan Rodney McCall was a charitable man – always doing his bit serving the local community. Once every week, he visited his mother-in-law to collect bread that had been donated at St Dorothy's Catholic Church in Glendora, California.

Always carefully displaying his handicapped driver's badge, Mr McCall parked on the street outside his mother-in-law's house for ten minutes, loading up the bread that was to be handed out to the homeless, hungry and needy of the local area.

A surprise, then, that Rodney was punished unfairly for this rare community spirit by the police authorities with a $40 fine for parking without a 'street permit' in front of his mother-in-law's home.

Mr McCall, who had previously lived in the same street for 35 years, thought, quite fairly, that the decision was 'insane'. 'I can't afford that,' he argued later. 'All I'm trying to do is help out the church but I guess no good deed goes unpunished.'

It appears that since 2004 street-parking permits have been required for each house in the street with each house being issued two parking passes free of charge. Visitors are reminded to borrow a permit or park in the resident's driveway during the restricted hours or face a fine. 'Mr McCall knew about the law, but his excuse was that he was only there for a short time,' Sgt Tim Staab said. 'Mr McCall took a chance and he got caught.' Mr McCall appealed, but the Glendora police department was unrepentant.

Sgt Staab added that the parking restrictions are well posted on the Glendora streets and if a car is unattended, the police have to abide by the laws the city council decide.

Let's just hope that this doesn't put off good Samaritans from doing their charity work.

GOOD WORKS – IF YOU DRIVE A TOW-AWAY TRUCK

Moragh Gee, a volunteer community worker for the Camden Home-Start programme rarely receives any special appreciation for her work – such is the world we live in these days. However, one afternoon spent caring for a four-year-old child on Hampstead Heath changed all that. Unfortunately, it wasn't quite the attention she was after.

Mrs Gee, a pensioner who had been a volunteer for six years, had filled out the required paperwork – a visitor's parking permit – but was dismayed to return to her car later in the day just as it was being loaded onto a tow- truck for having being parked in a pay and display bay. Mrs Gee pleaded with the Camden tow-truck driver not to remove her car, but her pleas fell on deaf ears. 'I begged him not to take my car away,' said Mrs Gee. 'I told him I had to get this small child home but I might as well have been talking to a brick wall.' Mrs Gee had not realised that visitors' permits were not valid in pay and display bays.

Mrs Gee paid £200 for her car to be released from Camden car pound – an unacceptable amount considering Mrs Gee volunteers her help for free to the Home Start programme.

Jennifer Crisp, a Camden Home-Start administrator, said, 'It is hard for us to recruit volunteers and I would understand if Mrs Gee said that she could not afford to volunteer any more. The driver saw it was an old lady, with a young child, and yet still took the car away. It is absolutely heartless.'

Mrs Gee wrote to Camden Council asking for the fee to be refunded, but heard nothing for weeks. However, Camden Council chiefs agreed to refund £150 of the £200 release fee.

HAMPERED BY A PARKING TICKET

Christmas 'tis the season to be jolly.

'Tis also the season to show 'goodwill towards all men and women'. Unfortunately, parking-ticket wardens sometimes put an unseasonal spanner in the works.

Charity worker Roger Hetherington stopped his car out- side Women's Aid, a sanctuary for abused women, to distribute food hampers – a much appreciated and helpful, local service when, well, you can guess what happens next. A parking attendant came along and issued him with a £60 parking fine.

Women's Aid appealed against the ticket and asked for it to be cancelled. 'We have been fighting for funding this year as it is,' their spokesperson stated, 'so we don't want to have to find money to pay parking tickets.'

DID YOU KNOW?
THE LONDON CONGESTION CHARGE (PART 1)

The London Congestion charge was introduced on 17th February 2003. The initial daily charge was £5. Two years later it was increased to £8 a day and in January 2011 that was increased to £10 per day. From 16th June 2014 it got a bit complicated. The daily charge was £11.50 if paid on the day you travelled and £14 if you paid the next day.

You can also for a fee, register for a Credit Card Autopay that automatically charges you a reduced daily charge of £10.50. Phew!!

Crime Doesn't Pay

Crime doesn't pay. Whether you are guilty or innocent ... someone will end up paying for those crimes eventually. In the following cases, the fine is usually in the shape of a parking ticket.

IT CAN GET WORSE

Nobody is happy to get a parking ticket, so when delivery driver Dennis Williams had one slapped on his van he immediately threw the parking ticket down onto the pavement in disgust. Unfortunately for Dennis luck was not on his side that day. His outburst was spotted by a nearby street warden on litter patrol who fined Mr Williams on the spot for being a litterbug!

Mr Williams was convicted at Carmarthen Magistrates Court and fined £150 – a tidy little sum that will, in Mr Dennis Williams' mind at least, be a little reminder to keep Britain tidy.

WHAT IS IT ABOUT PARKING METERS? (PART ONE)

What is it about parking meters that makes them just so appealing to steal? For British students, it's traffic cones – if only because they make funny hats – but for two New England pranksters stealing parking meters was their thing. This time though their cheeky stunt backfired and they were caught red-handed and summoned to the courtroom.

Christopher Puffer – aged 21 – pleaded guilty to a Class B charge of criminal mischief. He was arrested by New Hampshire Liquor Enforcement officers for removing a parking meter. He was also charged with criminal mischief for damaging the meter, which cost the city $288.26 to repair. In exchange for a reduced charge, Puffer negotiated a guilty plea. Casey Lee, Puffer's 22- year-old co-conspirator reached an identical agreement with the prosecution on the basis that both men had no previous convictions.

The judge imposed fines of $250, with $50 penalty assessments, to both men and ordered each to pay half the cost of repairing and re-installing the parking meter.

The parking meter dropped all charges of assault.

WHAT IS IT ABOUT PARKING METERS? (PART TWO)

Two teenagers in Sydney, Australia were arrested after setting fire to five parking meters.

Patrolling police officers in Bondi Junction found the meters alight and called the fire brigade. Not long after, police stopped a red Mazda 121 Sedan in the area and arrested the 17- and 18-year-old youths.

The boys were taken to a local police station for questioning. The first one being 'Why?'

WHERE'S THE PARKING METER?

In a story sounding not too dissimilar to the hilarious misadventures of Inspector Clouseau in the Pink Panther movies comes 'The Case of the Missing Parking Meters'. In Hanover, New Hampshire the police force had been confronted with a new – and very unlikely nemesis – a serial parking-meter thief. Or possibly thieves.

After eight parking meters were stolen in a local area, the police began investigating these mysterious disappearings. They increased their area patrols, remaining extra vigilant and commenced using hidden cameras to try to catch the guilty parties. Eventually, the police squad arrested a Vermont couple, and charged them with stealing eight parking meters containing as much as $3000 in change!

As a result of these 'vanishings', the city had noticed a remarkable drop in the amount of money they were collecting from meters. Over one five-week period officials estimated they lost up to $600 a week – certainly enough to give up the day job. Authorities later found several parking meters and the tools used to burgle them at the couple's home, evidence enough that the once elusive burglars had been caught red handed. 'The Case of the Missing Parking Meters' was finally solved.

> **DID YOU KNOW?**
>
> **THE LONDON CONGESTION CHARGE (PART 2)**
>
> In November 2006 Transport for London were issuing 20,000 Congestion Charge penalties each week. The face value of the penalty notices was £2 million.

NOW THAT'S WHAT I CALL A PARKING TICKET!

Parking tickets are, it's sad to say, a part of modern life. Most of us will at one point or another receive a parking ticket – if not more. Perhaps the most we will ever tally up is £100. One motorist, one very careless driver it must be said, ran up fines totalling a staggering £59,100!

The green Iveco heavy-goods lorry with registration number G375NKK had run up 384 Penalty Charge Notices (PCNs) for allegedly breaking parking regulations in Camden. The vehicle and its owner were being hunted by officials at Camden Council's offices and was eventually spotted in Queen's Crescent and removed.

It was due to be sold at auction and the proceeds used against the amount owed to the council.

Apparently, the vehicle, along with a further two vehicles, had been fraudulently registered to a man living in North London.

The council had been using new technology, such as parking attendants' handheld computers, to help success- fully track down persistent evaders. It was also searching for other vehicles including a yellow Iveco heavy-goods vehicle-registration number R505 ODC and a yellow and red Iveco heavy-goods vehicle, M354 GVK.

The council continues to search for the worst parking offenders, in particular seeking to track down the 'Top 10' parking-fine evaders.

The council even published a telephone number for members of the public who see the vehicles to report them to council staff.

PARKING PROBLEM

When Stephanie Bradley-Wilson got her licence suspended for having an unpaid parking ticket she was more than surprised – she was flabbergasted.

Why? Because she's the Madison Police Lieutenant in charge of the city's traffic and parking enforcement! Her licence was suspended when the Department of Motor Vehicles (DMV) was incorrectly told that she had an outstanding parking fine.

In truth, she had sent in her money but because of a 'computer error' it wasn't correctly applied to her ticket. To make matters worse, Ms Bradley-Wilson was just one of a number of people who found themselves victims of the software error that not only failed to record payments of fines that had been paid but also, somewhat cheekily I might say, added unjustified late-payment penalties, resulting in some people having their licence registration revoked.

'It happens,' a spokesperson for the DMV said. 'It used to be human error, but now it's a combination sometimes of human and software error.'

Apology accepted!

HOW NOT TO FIGHT YOUR PARKING TICKET

Fighting a parking ticket can be pretty daunting. In some countries you appear in court, in others, before an adjudicator. So, if you get a parking ticket how do you fight it?

In Cyprus, driving instructor Andis Kyriakides (Mr K) fought his parking ticket in a rather unusual way. The story starts when traffic warden Andreas Stavrou (Mr S) told Mr K to move his car as it was parked close to a roundabout – the roads were incidentally closed off during a demonstration.

Mr K moved his car to a nearby street where he again parked it illegally. His car was then spotted by the traffic police who towed it away. This is where the appeal process took a rather, shall we say, unusual turn.

Mr K was furious and blamed Mr S for what had happened. He then went looking for Mr S's car which was parked near the traffic wardens' offices in Nicosia. It was then that another traffic warden observed Mr K scratching the side of Mr S's car with his own car key.

The police were called and Mr K was arrested. Mr K found himself in court where he decided not to appeal against the parking ticket and to plead guilty to causing £250 worth of damage.

Mr S told the court that he had been satisfactorily compensated for the damage to his car and did not have any complaints against the defendant. Despite this, the judge sentenced Mr K to three months' imprisonment! The judge said, 'The fact that the defendant is a mature citizen of our community and has a clean record before the incident can only shorten the sentence but is not enough to constitute a lesser punishment of a suspended sentence, as requested by the defence.'

Some legal observers described the court's decision as 'quite harsh'.

PARKING TICKETS ARE GOOD FOR YOU

Family comes first, so the saying goes,
but not according to Maria Brunner from
Munich in Germany.

When Maria got a £50 parking ticket she decided against paying and, instead, chose to spend three months in jail. Why? To get away from her husband and children!

'I don't mind being sent to jail,' Maria said. 'It means I can finally get some rest and relaxation without having to cook, wash and clean for everyone at home.'

Maria waved to her friends and smiled as the police led her away.

UNPAID PARKING TICKET? GET HANDCUFFED AND LOCKED UP

There is always someone who – no matter how old – has to be made an example of.

When 97-year-old Harriette Kelton was stopped by police for having an out-of-date registration and MOT they discovered there was a warrant out for her arrest for non- payment on an existing parking ticket. Without any commotion, the OAP was handcuffed and taken to jail.

Mrs Kelton, a former schoolteacher from Dallas, Texas, was in police custody for about two hours before her lawyer arrived and organised a release. Her son, District Judge David Kelton, said it would be 'inappropriate' for him to discuss the arrest.

Mrs Kelton's other son, Dr Phil Kelton, however, felt compelled to speak and complained that the police did not use 'real judgement' incarcerating her, considering the lady's age and health concerns. A police spokesman fought back claiming the arresting officers had 'no choice but to arrest'.

Clearly Mrs Kelton had to be arrested just in case she grew up to be a hardened criminal!

PARKING SCAM

London gangsters are renowned for having their fingers in all sorts of pies –have become a tasty, lucrative treat. And in a city where gun crime is on the rise – and parking costs an arm and leg anyway – it seems that's not all people stand to lose.

In 2006 London police uncovered a £1 million scam involving thieves using counterfeit keys to open the loaded "old style" parking meters and simply walking off with the riches. Most London tourists and commuters often wince at how expensive inner-city parking is, so it's no surprise that gangsters want in on the loot – a metaphorical sitting duck. Police revealed that competition between gangs to control the scam had become so violent that one man was murdered!

The Westminster borough was London's worst-affected area for parking-meter thefts but other councils were not immune. A police source reported, 'There is a huge amount of money in parking meters every day due to the cost of pay and display. This has obviously attracted some serious criminals who are prepared to kill if necessary to secure their territory.'

The loot – mostly in coins – was untraceable, making this a very attractive crime. Because of the problem Westminster and other councils phased out the use of marking meters and introduced pay and display systems and pay by phone and pay by text parking.

FEELING BLUE OVER STOLEN BLUE BADGE

Disabled drivers often find themselves the victims of crime. Their blue, disabled badges – ironically put on display for the wardens – become all too irresistible for devious characters with bad intentions. Well, one such character ended up in a whole heap of trouble. And in court.

Fazlur Chowdhury, a Croydon resident and able driver, bought a stolen disabled blue badge that he intended to use for less-than-honourable purposes. However, in a clever sting by Wandsworth Council's undercover fraud team, Mr Chowdhury was caught red-handed on film using the badge to park nearer his office in Nightingale Lane, Clapham. Mr Chowdhury admitted to four counts of using the badge fraudulently.

At South Western Magistrates' Court, the judge heard how the original badge owner had her car broken into in East London. Yet again, it's a case of crime doesn't pay – you do. The defendant was fined a total of £3,000 and ordered to pay all court costs.

The icing on the cake? Mr Chowdhury also had to pay an additional £190 to get his car back after it was seized as part of the council's sting operation.

SCAM-ALOT!

Shocked that even parking attendants have been seduced by the dark side of the law? Well, don't be.

Revelations made by a BBC undercover documentary revealed in 2006 how some of London's less morally concerned parking attendants were being bribed to cancel parking-ticket notices.

The BBC undercover reporter – let's call him Mr X for no other reason than because it sounds cool – found a string of rackets involving attendants in several of London's boroughs.

Mr X – a journalist who spent more than four months working as a parking attendant – caught his shamed colleagues on camera as they issued illegal tickets and took bribes and backhanders to settle parking tickets and clamp- release fees – finally confirming many London motorists' suspicions that something fishy and underhand was going on.

Among the many shenanigans Mr X caught was a parking attendant, working for the council's contractor, who was filmed taking £25 from a second reporter, posing as a

minicab driver, to cancel a £100 parking ticket in Camden. The cheeky scamp.

Another warden was filmed teaching our Mr X how to illegally increase the number of fines he issued after he was warned by his bosses for not issuing the 'required' ten tickets a day.

The BBC said the investigation was triggered when a 'whistleblower' contacted them.

As a result of the programme the two contracting firms whose staff were implicated in the undercover operation launched a full-scale investigation. One claimed not to have found any evidence to support the BBC's claims, believing that the incidents were 'isolated events'.

(The author gave technical advice to the BBC production team during the year it took to produce this documentary)

HOW TO GET A HERNIA

We've all seen Ocean's Eleven. Bank robbing is cool – that's if you're stupid enough to do it. One such bank robber from Germany tried his luck and very nearly had everyone fooled.

This particular story emerged in Aachen, after a clerk received a prison sentence of four years for stealing €1 million from his employers. In coins! In coins! It was reported the number of coins stolen was 1.2 million – equal (in bulk) to 26 people weighing 11 stone each!

A court spokesperson recalled how the 39-year-old man stole bags of coins, collected from the city's 330 parking ticket machines, and given to him for checking. The clerk would later convert the cash into notes and pay the money into various different bank accounts, leaving – he thought - an untraceable trail.

And he did. In fact, it was only after Aachen City council started bypassing the clerk by paying its parking revenues directly into the bank that officials realised something was afoot.

'All of a sudden the revenues from the ticket machines shot up dramatically so it became obvious there was a big hole in the accounts,' a bank spokesperson said, coining a phrase.

The clerk learned his lesson – and you can bank on him not forgetting it.

DID YOU KNOW?

THE FIRST UK PARKING TICKET

The first person to receive a parking ticket in the UK was Doctor Thomas Creighton on 19th September 1960 when he parked his Ford Popular outside a West End hotel while attending to a patient suffering from a heart attack. There was a public outcry when the facts became known and the doctor was let off the £2 fine.

IT'S GOOD TO GET A PARKING TICKET

It may be hard to believe but Robert Comeau was counting his blessings – and good fortune – when he received a $50 parking ticket! Mr Comeau, a member of the Canadian Forces, was working at a hotel and decided to stay overnight. In the morning, to his horror, he discovered that his 1999 Toyota Tercel had been stolen. He called the police immediately and reported the theft.

However, having given up hope of ever finding his vehicle, he was surprised to receive in the post a parking ticket issued at the University of Ottawa Sports Complex.

Mr Comeau contacted the Ottawa police but was told that they wouldn't be able to check on the car. So, Mr Comeau decided to do some detective work of his own and went to the university parking lot.

Sure enough there was his car, though unfortunately not in the condition he had kept it in – the front-door locks had been broken, and all manner of junk (crack pipes, liquor bottles, etc.) had been dumped inside.

An incredibly pleased Mr Comeau was happy to have found his car even though it was all thanks to the parking ticket. He was even happier when the university authorities cancelled the ticket.

However, he wasn't so keen on the thought of cleaning the car!

HYPOCRITICAL TICKETAL

Keith Bee, a former policeman, had every right to be buzzed off!

Earlier in the morning Mr Bee, had received a parking ticket in the post and when spotting the opportune moment decided to take the law into his own hands. Having spotted a parking warden's official van, with its white livery, amber roof light and 'parking enforcement' logos in a loading bay in Doncaster town centre, Mr Bee was certain the vehicle had been left there illegally and began salivating at the prospect of a warden having to ticket his own vehicle.

To his astonishment, Mr Bee watched as the parking attendant left the illegally parked vehicle and walked down the street to check on other illegally parked vehicles. Mr Bee launched an immediate counter-sting by finding another nearby parking attendant and casually pointed out that his colleague had broken the very same law he was employed to serve. Mr Bee watched as the ticket was printed out and left on the vehicle – and took a photograph to make sure it was done correctly.

Doncaster Council's spokesman for crime and public safety later commented that 'all vehicles that break parking laws, including those that are council owned, are issued with tickets to keep drivers and pedestrians safe and traffic moving smoothly. In line with his training, the attendant issued a ticket to defuse a potential confrontation.'

How did the council make sure that the parking ticket was paid?

> **INTERNATIONAL UNPAID PARKING TICKETS (PART 1)**
>
> According to the Guardian newspaper at April 2017 in the Australian capital city of Canberra, foreign diplomats owed more than A$500,000 (£290,000), most of which was unpaid parking fines.

Appeals

It's a basic human right to feel hard done by ... the legal system is based around it. No longer do you have to take your punishment like a man though – you can appeal! Chances are you might get off. Although with some mean parking attendants you'll be trying your luck!

PAY AND DISCOURAGE

Do you think that pay and display prices are exorbitant? Well, one Toronto man has proof.

When Tom Nolan put his credit card in the machine to pay for his pay-and-display voucher the machine churned it out just fine. But when Mr Nolan examined it carefully it showed a receipt for $57,806.45 on one side and a different charge for $152.54 on the other.

An astonished Mr Nolan said that he immediately called his credit-card company who confirmed that there was nothing to worry about as his credit limit was not that high.

According to the Toronto Parking Authority the glitch in the machine probably occurred because of the cold weather.

BETTER OR VERSE?

You appeal your parking ticket and get a reply – but do you expect it in verse?

Andrew Lynch was not happy when he got a £30 parking ticket while on holiday in Keswick, Cumbria. So he wrote an appeal to the council.

He was surprised to receive a reply (who wouldn't be!) from the council's finance director. With a difference. The letter started:

'Park only and wholly in a clearly marked bay. That's what the signs in the car park say.'

Hoping that poetry would soften her heart Mr Lynch replied in a similar poetic vein. But it fell on unromantic ears and the ticket was not cancelled.

In a subsequent statement, the council apologised for their 'lovely' letter. 'No offence was intended by the tone of the letter and we fully understand that not everyone would appreciate the light-hearted nature of the response. We clearly accept and apologise for the approach taken as inappropriate.'

'This person clearly has too much time on her hands,' came Mr Lynch's dignified response.

SIGN OF THE TIMES

Many a motorist has claimed with some justification that parking signs are unclear, but most do not pursue the matter. Barry Mitchell is one motorist who did.

Mr Mitchell was taken to court for not paying a parking ticket he received in Heene Road, Worthing.

Appearing at Worthing Magistrates' Court, 63-year-old Mr Mitchell told prosecutors before his trial that the parking ticket was unfair due to the 'ambiguous meaning' of the parking signs. He then presented them with a bulky dossier detailing the various interpretations of the signs, which are placed throughout Worthing. Mr Mitchell's argument is that there are three valid interpretations of the signs, which anyone would agree is two interpretations too many!

After reading through the papers, the court told Mr Mitchell the prosecution was not proceeding with the case against him.

The implications if the court had ruled the signs were in fact unclear would create a legal precedent considering thousands of people have been given tickets – at £30 a time – for up to ten years since the signs were put up.

Of course, the council inevitably disagreed. 'We believe they fully conform with national requirements and are consistent with parking legislation and the Highway Code.'

Sounds like the council may have to brush up on their sign language!

NO TRUCK WITH PARKING TICKETS

There are all sorts of ways to dispute parking tickets but some motorists have used, let's just say, 'unusual' methods.

When Michelle Traverse saw that her car was about to be towed away she picked up her seven-month old baby, ran from her Hampstead flat, jumped into the tow truck and refused to budge until the police came!

Ms Traverse, while on maternity leave of all things, had not spotted a temporary sign on a lamppost in Parkhill Road indicating that parking bays were out of use until December due to a major gas leak.

The tow-truck driver ordered Ms Traverse out of the truck but resorted to calling the police when she refused to move. Eventually, a distressed Ms Traverse called her mother, who came and forked out £200 from her credit card to have the car released after the police drove them to the car pound.

We should have no truck with clampers.

Wardens

Traffic Wardens have different names all over the world. Some have meaningless official titles, and some are just meaningless. Many we have heard are rude and some coincidentally rhyme with 'anchor'. Whatever you call them, the overzealousness of some traffic wardens remains the same …

HUNG, DRAWN AND QUARTERED

Saving money for a rainy day is one thing. Stealing $120,000 in quarters from parking meters is another thing entirely!

Vincent Howard, a former parking-meter attendant from Detroit, pleaded guilty to abusing his position for financial gain. Howard worked for the city of Mount Clemens for 23 years but was arrested after police raided his home and found thousands of dollars in coins! Investigators also found money in Howard's car and the car he used on his rounds. Mr Howard had admitted taking $500 every two weeks for 10 years.

Unsurprisingly, in court Mr Howard was ordered to pay most of the money back. A judge also saw fit to put the offender on an electronic tether for six months just in case he got any other bright ideas!

PUNCHING HIS TICKET

When Tim Hudson saw a parking attendant's vehicle parked illegally he thought it was a photo opportunity too good to be missed. Using his mobile-phone camera to take pictures of the attendant's illegally parked vehicle, the snap-happy parking paparazzo enjoyed the irony of the warden getting a taste of his own medicine.

However, Mr Hudson's actions didn't meet with the approval of parking attendant Alfred Damete-Kumi. So much so, Mr Damete-Kumi punched Mr Hudson's mobile- phone camera out of his hands!

As with most solutions to life's problems, fisticuffs didn't work. Damete-Kumi, 58, ended up in Camberwell Green Magistrates' Court and was found guilty of causing criminal damage. He was given a 12-month conditional discharge, fined £100 and ordered to pay £120 to Mr Hudson – a knockout result for Mr Hudson.

However, this was one fight the warden didn't win!

PARKING IS JUST FINE FOR SOME

Passengers who fly from Austin Straubel International Airport regularly paid through the nose to keep their cars parked at the airport. What they didn't know was that some of their money ended up in Rebecca Eland's pocket.

Ms Eland pleaded no contest to theft by false representation after she was accused of stealing $100,000 from the airport's parking operation.

Investigators reported that Ms Eland had stolen the money while working as an airport parking attendant in 2004 by retaining the validation ticket stubs and pocketing the money drivers paid as they left the airport's parking lots.

Although, from the sounds of it now, that's the lot for Ms Eland!

PARKING-TICKET BLITZ

The history books are full of amazing achievements. But one man has achieved a record few of us would applaud.

Manchester city parking attendant Damien Smethurst, on a motorcycle no less, achieved a remarkable record when he issued a mind-blowing 101 parking tickets! There was just one tiny problem: 84 of the 101 parking tickets he issued were wrong! Doh!

Mr Smethurst handed out £8,080 worth of fines – that's one for nearly every 7 minutes on a Bank Holiday Monday when in Manchester at that time parking on a single yellow line was actually allowed!

A blushing Manchester City Council cancelled the parking tickets and offered the ticketed motorists a day's free parking in the city centre.

The local contractor, Control Plus, who employed Mr Smethurst said, 'It is beyond belief. This is what gives all parking attendants a bad name.

A Manchester City Council spokesperson said 'We are aware that Control Plus has carried out its own internal investigation into this matter, resulting in both the parking attendant and his supervisor being interviewed. In this case no disciplinary action was taken.'

The council subsequently issued the parking contract to another contractor.

A PENNY FOR YOUR THOUGHTS

Jean Jacques Carquillat had had enough when he received two parking tickets on the same day. So much so, it prompted him to have an exciting idea.

The Canadian restaurateur decided to fight back and, quite literally, spend a penny. Eight thousand to be exact! In a bizarre turn up for the books, Mr Carquillat turned up at Kingston town hall and made a special delivery, not a delivery of mouth-watering gourmet food from his restaurant, but boxes containing 8,000 pennies to pay for the $80 he owed the local council.

Joan Brandt, head of the city's Parking Violations Bureau, wondered how Mr Carquillat would react if city employees paid for meals at his restaurant with pennies. 'How would he like that?' she asked sourly.

Mr Carquillat would be delighted, you would assume. He could use them to pay for future parking tickets!

(Note: The city held a parking-ticket amnesty in September 2006. This was part of an effort to collect $450,000 in outstanding fines that had mounted up since 1994. However, only $6505 was paid during the two-week programme, city officials said.)

PAY YOUR PARKING TICKET!

Have you ever forgotten to pay a parking ticket? If so, what did you do about it?

William Fogarty in the USA had forgotten to pay his parking ticket – in 1946!

Mr Fogarty received the parking ticket while his black 1935 Ford coupé was parked outside a cinema in Norfolk, Virginia. He promptly bought a $1 money order to pay the fine. But he was discharged from the Navy soon afterward, and somehow forgot that the money order was still in his wallet.

Amazingly, Mr Fogarty, an 86-year-old Palm Harbor retiree, found the parking ticket as he was looking through a box of memorabilia from his Navy days. He discovered a leather wallet that had first belonged to his younger brother. Mr Fogarty carried the wallet after his brother, Edward, was killed in World War II. Sure enough, there inside the wallet was the $1 money order.

Mr Fogarty immediately wrote to the Norfolk police and enclosed his debt. The money order was dated 14 May, 1946. 'I hope you will forgive me the long delay in sending it to you,' his letter began.

Norfolk Police Officer Chris Amos said Mr Fogarty's money would not be cashed, but instead sent to the Police Department's museum, where it would be framed and displayed.

'It's one of those things that restores your faith in mankind,' Officer Amos said.

> INTERNATIONAL UNPAID PARKING TICKETS (PART 2)
>
> In 2016, Boris Johnson told Members of Parliament that in London, diplomatic missions and international organisations had failed to pay 4,858 parking fines totaling £477,499 of which £161,328, was later waived or paid.

In Sickness and in Health

It seems that some mean parking attendants think that the cure to being ill is the prescription of a parking ticket. They couldn't be more wrong ...

AN ACCIDENT WAITING TO HAPPEN

You're in a car accident. You get whiplash. You've got to go to hospital. This was the scenario that one poor female driver found herself in, in Hammersmith in 2006. As the ambulance took her to hospital, the police took away her car.

So far, so unfortunate. But when the driver was released from hospital, there was a problem: the police couldn't remember where they'd put the car. By the time they found it, four days later round the back of Paddington Green Police Station, it was littered with parking tickets.

When the driver complained about the five £100 tickets, Westminster Council initially rejected her appeal. Eventually the Metropolitan Police apologised, blamed an administrative error for the situation, and the council cancelled the tickets.

Another fine mess.

OUT ON A LIMB

Some parking tickets cost an arm and a leg. None more so than for the following unlucky motorist ...

Disabled driver Peter Stapleton was driving along when his artificial leg fell off, forcing him to pull over to the kerb to try and fix it.

Fortunately (you would think!) there was a parking attendant nearby. Mr Stapleton told the attendant about the unattached limb and that he would require a visit to a friend's flat nearby – for about 10 minutes – to re- attach the leg. The attendant confirmed that no ticket would be issued.

So, it came as a complete surprise, and to Mr Stapleton's complete horror, that a parking ticket was smiling back at him from underneath his windscreen wiper when he returned. A furious Mr Stapleton understandably refused to pay the fine, resulting in the costs spiralling to £465.

After lengthy to-ing and fro-ing, the council subsequently reduced the fine to £100 – a small, if shallow, victory.

A NASTY OPERATION

Dr Graeme Pogrel was used to surprises when dealing with patients, but nothing prepared him for the surprise he got when he was given a parking ticket even though his car displayed clearly a 'Doctor on Duty' sticker!

OPERATION DUMB AND DUMBER

When the driver of a vehicle owned by a plastic-window company amusingly called 'Plastic Surgeons' found a parking space at the local hospital he was delighted. Happiness turned to astonishment when he got a parking ticket for parking in the wrong car park.

The parking attendant told him, 'You are a plastic surgeon; you should be in the staff car-parking area, not the visitors' car park.'

As the driver said, 'If I were a plastic surgeon I'd be driving a Ferrari, not an old van!'

The parking contractors said that they would investigate the matter. Perhaps they should investigate the cost of a brain transplant for the parking attendant.

PARKING OPERATIONS

You would think that making sure a hospital cancer consultant got to hospital on time was important. Well, not for one bunch of car clampers.

Doctor Paul Thiruchelvam, a hospital cancer consultant, was on his way to hospital to operate on seriously ill patients when a heartless clamper clamped his car. The clamper used the clamp to disable the car, over a single parking ticket issued in March 2006 that Dr Thiruchelvam had appealed against. The clamper refused to release the vehicle unless he paid £863 on the spot!

Dr Thiruchelvam said, 'It was daylight robbery. I was told to "put up or shut up". I explained to him I was a doctor and I had to leave immediately because I needed to operate on cancer patients but he didn't care. He said he was going to tow my car and sell it at auction.'

One word: Unbelievable.

IS THERE A DOCTOR IN THE HOUSE?

Some years ago Buckinghamshire County Council appear to have had their priorities all mixed up.

Moments after Doctor Ewan Bumpstead's Peugeot was smashed into by suspected joyriders, he was ticketed for blocking a footpath. How crazy is that? To make matters even more unbearable, Dr Bumpstead was making a house call to an elderly patient who required treatment.

Buckinghamshire County Council 'officials' responded that it was more important to punish Dr Bumpstead for blocking a footpath regardless of the accident. 'Anybody who wanted to use the path would have to walk in the mud to get around' the insensitive council responded.

Thankfully, the doctor was not in his car when it was hit, but that didn't seem to make much difference to the local council officials.

HEART ATTACK

Whilst David Holmes was driving along he felt chest pains. He immediately drove himself to hospital. When he arrived there, he was forced to park on the road and was treated for a heart attack. A kind nurse left a note on the windscreen saying it was an emergency and that David's daughter would pick up the car later. Amazingly despite the note a pitiless parking attendant slapped a parking ticket on David's car.

It's enough to give you another heart attack. Despite an appeal to the local council, the £40 fine was not cancelled.

NURSING A COMPLAINT!

District nurse Nicky Willetts, from Sutton Coldfield, was left seething after a traffic warden gave her a £60 parking ticket … while delivering medical equipment to a patient's home! Is there no justice anymore? Surely, medical staff should be exempt from such blatant outrageous ticketing?

SICK TICKETED

Doctors in Leeds doctors got very sick – sick of parking tickets!

The problem started when Leeds City Council changed its parking regulations. It introduced residents-only parking and painted double yellow lines over three doctors' parking bays at the Ashton View surgery.

Since then staff and patients have been issued with parking tickets constantly.

Following the change, the surgery's twelve staff have only four spaces available whilst the surgery's 2,800 patients face a lengthy walk to get to their appointments. A ridiculous situation.

'It is a terrible state when I cannot even park in front of the surgery where I treat sick patients,' Dr Solomon Wong recently commented. 'Even the patients are receiving tickets! It is the last thing they need to be thinking of when they come to see the doctor.' You would think!

Councillor Bernard Atha (Labour, Kirkstall) said: 'It seems this is a cash cow for the council and totally unfair.'

> DID YOU KNOW?
>
> A ROSE BY ANY OTHER NAME
>
> We all know what a parking ticket is but throughout the UK and the rest of the rest of the world they are sometimes called different things. In the UK the correct legal name for a council- issued parking ticket is a Penalty Charge Notice (sometimes referred to as a PCN). In places where a parking ticket is still a criminal offence it is called a Fixed Penalty Notice that can only be fought in court.

Just Bonkers

Bonkers adjective: mad; crazy. The origin of the word bonkers may be unknown but the following stories could be the key to finding out ...

DEATH, TAXES ... AND PARKING TICKETS

US founding father Benjamin Franklin once wrote, 'In this world nothing can be said to be certain, except death and taxes.' But now you must add parking tickets.

Taxpayers in Aylesbury knew that they had to pay their taxes. One 31 January, the last day for submission of their tax returns, many taxpayers went to the Inland Revenue offices in Kingfisher Exchange, parked briefly and dropped off their tax returns only to find their vehicles clamped.

In order for the motorists' cars to be released they had to pay a £120 fine. Ironically the fine for late delivery of your tax return was £100.

A STICKY PROBLEM

A driver in Worcester found himself in a sticky situation earlier this year, thanks to the lack of adhesive on the car park ticket he'd bought.

Having paid £1.50 to park for three hours in Croft Road car park, Robert Haywood discovered that his parking ticket did not have any stick to stick it to his windscreen. Leaving it on his dashboard, he thought no more about it, and went shopping with his wife.

But on his return, there was no sign of the ticket on the dashboard, but there was a different kind on the windscreen ... yep, you guessed it, a parking ticket. Mr Haywood's only conclusion was that as it was a particularly windy day, the wind must have somehow rocked the car and knocked the ticket off.

Mr Haywood 'stuck' to his guns, and his appeal against the ticket was successful.

SNOW MORE PARKING TICKETS

New York's first snow storm of 2007 deposited mountains of snow in New York streets.

The City's Sanitation Department quickly sent out its team of snow ploughs to clear streets but unfortunately this left thousands of cars buried by snow drifts with their owners unable to move them.

Despite the problem the city did not suspend its alternate- side-of-the-street parking regulations. Things then took a turn for the worst when later on traffic-enforcement officials slapped parking tickets on the stranded cars' windscreens.

Motorists protested and initially New York's then mayor said that the tickets had to be paid. However, after more protests, Mayor Michael Bloomberg agreed that the 4,000+ parking tickets would be cancelled.

WELCOME TO WARWICKSHIRE

Warwick is a beautiful part of England but it had no appeal for one man who received a parking ticket from the local council.

Krister Nylander was dismayed to receive a parking ticket in the post for parking in beautiful Warwick. But he knew the parking ticket was wrong because he lives in Sweden and had not visited England since he was 16. The offending vehicle was his 20-ton snowmobile which had never left his barn, let alone Sweden.

How did it get the ticket? I've absolutely no Ikea.

HELP FOR DOCTOR WHO

Followers of the BBC series Doctor Who might argue that the time travelling doctor (and his bevy of beautiful assistants!) needs all the help he can get to fight the dreaded Daleks – even though their Achilles heel would seemingly be as simple as a flight of stairs.

However, fiction fused with reality when a parking attendant ticketed a lorry on its way to the BBC Television Centre. Although this was no ordinary lorry ... strapped to its back was a 6-foot-high model Dalek!

The lorry's driver, Martin Wilkie, told the Sun newspaper: 'I couldn't believe it, I'd just nipped into a shop. The warden wouldn't back down.'

Surely even a parking-ticket attendant can see the funny side of ticketing a Dalek!

EX-TER-MIN-ATE!

COSTLY ADVICE

We've all got lost when driving and have stopped to ask a kind person the way.

When driver Derek Scott wanted directions, he thought, 'Who can help me? How about a nice friendly parking attendant?' Derek stopped to ask a parking attendant for directions but then Derek got more than he bargained for. Whilst he was getting directions the parking attendant's colleague slapped a £100 parking ticket on his car.

DOCTOR WHO'S NEW TIME MACHINE

One parking attendant, obviously a Doctor Who fan, mistook one vehicle for the famous Tardis Time Machine which, as we all know, is a lot bigger inside than out.

The parking attendant issued a parking ticket to a motorist claiming that he had not displayed a pay-and-display ticket. The motorist appealed insisting that he had.

Camden Council wrote back saying that the 'parking attendant had examined all the windows and looked in the vehicle and could not see a Pay & Display ticket'.

Only one problem: the vehicle was a motorbike!!

PARKING SPACE – THE FINAL FRONTIER

Star Trek's Captain Kirk would say the immortal words 'Beam me up Scotty' and a fraction of a second later he would be transported to another time and place.

Colin Southwell didn't have the benefit of Scotty's help, but it seemed that Islington Council did.

When a council letter arrived with a photo that showed Colin's van in a bus lane at 9.47 in the morning he was prepared to the pay the fine. But then he opened another council letter, which arrived in the same post, only to find that this fined him £100 for overstaying a meter one minute later at 9.48 – even though the meter was five minutes away. Knowing that his van could not travel at 150 miles per hour and that he could not be in two places at the same time he challenged the validity of the council's parking ticket.

It's ticketing, Jim, but not as we know it.

DRIVING YOU CRAZY

Driving instructors are pretty much used to the trials and tribulations of teaching people to drive. Three-point turns, as we all know, can be very tricky to learn. So, spare a thought for the driving instructor who got a CCTV parking ticket when his pupil stalled whilst attempting a three- point turn and could not restart the car! The offence? Parking more than 50 centimetres from the kerb.

Can someone please teach the camera operator how to do an emergency stop?

THE LONGEST-EVER PARKING APPEAL

New Zealander Ian Fraser's nightmare started when he received a letter telling him he had an unpaid parking fine for an 'unspecified offence'. Mr Fraser was very surprised as he knew nothing about the so called 'offence' and wrote back saying so.

He then received another letter from the Justice Ministry informing him of a $115 fine for a 1994 parking offence in Dunedin! But – Mr Fraser had never owned a car with the licence plate mentioned in the letter and he hadn't been to Dunedin in 28 years.

He was then threatened with arrest for refusing to pay the fine so he approached the media, the Justice Minister, opposition MPs, Dunedin's mayor and local police for help. Eventually Dunedin's Mayor, Peter Chin, said that no payment was required because the original parking ticket was so old, council staff had been unable to find how the ticket came to be in Mr Fraser's name.

He ended the letter by saying, 'I hope this experience has not put you off visiting Dunedin in the future. Twenty- eight years is too long to stay away.'

Not for Mr Fraser it wasn't!

IT'S CURTAINS FOR YOU

Master curtain maker Barry Gilby takes great pride in the beautiful curtains that he makes and one day was on his way to deliver some to one of his clients. He saw that there was a space on the other side of the road where he could park, and because he was unloading his vehicle he knew that it was safe to do so. What was even better (or so he thought) was the fact that were two parking attendants right next to the place he was going to park and there they were chatting away. 'Great,' he thought, but little did he realise that this was to be anything but.

He parked his van and said to one of the parking attendants, 'Look, I'm delivering these curtains to the flat opposite and I'll be back to pick up the rails, etc. As you can see I'm unloading so that's all right, isn't it?' The parking attendant said yes it was.

So off Barry went, proudly carrying the curtains, and a few minutes later came back to collect the curtain rail. To his horror he saw a parking ticket slapped smack bang on the windscreen.

He chased after the parking attendant he had spoken to and said, 'I spoke to you. I said I was unloading and you said it was OK, yet now you've given me a parking ticket. Why?' The parking attendant replied, 'I didn't give you the parking ticket, it was my mate.'

It was curtains for Barry when the parking attendants went off the rails – but the parking attendants should have pulled themselves together.

FEELING RUN DOWN

Are you feeling run down? Well, but for the quick reflexes of Adrian Porter, you would have been if you were one of the pedestrians who dashed in front of Adrian's car as he was crossing a yellow box junction.

Mr Porter had to pull up sharply in the box to avoid the two pedestrians. To his horror the next day Mr Porter received a penalty charge notice in the post for 'stopping on a junction box whilst prohibited'. For some reason the 'live' operator operating the box-junction camera did not seem to see the pedestrians who are clearly shown in the photo which accompanied the penalty charge, and processed the penalty.

As Mr Porter asked 'Am I supposed to run down the person in front of the car? The council seems to think you should.'

OFFSIDE, REF!

You're coming up to the goal, you're ready to shoot the ball into net when the referee calls a halt. Not because you're offside or have done some shirt pulling, but because you're going to get a parking ticket.

At two Sunday League matches in Bolton referees blew their whistles early when five parking wardens and two policemen arrived and threatened car parkers with tickets. No one was spared as players, spectators and officials at the matches – Greyman against Gypsie Tent and Jolly Waggoner against Morris Dancers – had to race to their cars to avoid getting ticketed on a stretch of Spa Road in Bolton, next to the two Queen's Park football pitches.

Bob Shuttleworth, the League's general secretary, said: 'The referees had to blow their whistles early for full-time and it was like the start of the Le Mans 24-hour race as everybody started running to their cars.'

Red cards all round for the traffic wardens.

> **DID YOU KNOW?**
>
> **CONFUSING PARKING SIGNS**
>
> Many Los Angeles streets have multiple signs. For example, on a single corner there may be three signs: No Parking 4-7, 15 Minute Parking 8-4. No Parking Tuesday.

(Un)Common Sense

The word 'sense' is often joined with 'common'. But in many of the following stories in this chapter the only 'common' theme is nonsense.

BAD NEWS COMES IN TREES

If a tree fell on your car, you and your family – having escaped death by mere inches – would think that things could only get better. Well, for one woman they got decidedly worse.

Nicky Clegg from Stoulton, near Pershore, was driving along the Bromwich Road with her 82-year-old mother and her 11-year-old son when without warning a tree crashed on her car. Miraculously they escaped unhurt but the car ended up with a crushed bonnet, smashed windscreen and broken wing mirrors.

Police dragged the wrecked car to the side of the road and told Nicky that it was fine to leave it there and she could pick it up the following day. But when Nicky came back the next day, she was astonished to find a parking ticket on the window.

This is a story with a good news/bad news ending. The good news: the council eventually cancelled the ticket.

The bad news: to add insult to injury, someone broke into the car and stole the stereo.

A MOURNFUL TALE

Whilst mourners paid their respects, four cars in the funeral cortege were given parking tickets. Officials of the funeral directors, Leverton & Sons (who in 1997 conducted Princess Diana's funeral), said they tried to stop the parking attendant from issuing parking tickets to two of the vehicles, but without success.

A Westminster Council spokesman insisted that the parking attendant had acted in accordance with the law, then stated 'Ticketing a funeral procession is obviously not ideal.'

That's one way of putting it.

A SICK JOKE

Ailing children are always a worry, so it was understandable that when Laurie Ward's child became ill and started vomiting, it made her late back to her car. When she did get back to her car she got something else to turn the stomach – a you-know-what.

She appealed to Brighton council who sent her a 'light- hearted' letter telling her they were scrapping the fine with the additional words: 'Please make sure your daughter only vomits within pay and display time.'

Laurie was definitely not amused. She told the Daily Mirror: 'It was an attempt at humour. This is not the way I expect to be treated by a public body.'

Someone from Brighton Council needs to go for a lie down.

PARKING BLITZ ON WEDDING BLISS

The stunning bride and handsome groom had exchanged their vows at a wonderful wedding ceremony. The bridal car was beautifully decorated with ribbons and flowers, ready to whisk them away. What could go wrong?

After the ceremony, bride Lisa Williamson and her groom Andrew left the registry office and returned to their bridal car to find it festooned not with 'Just Married' signs or the traditional tin cans but ... a non- traditional parking ticket!

Andrew told the Sheffield Star, 'When we went to the town hall to register the wedding, we were told that we could park one wedding car outside ... how could a traffic warden not notice that it was decorated as a bridal car?'

CRAZY AND WICKED

Carers who devote their lives to looking after disabled relatives are society's unsung heroes. They are owed an enormous debt of thanks ... which they seldom get.

Imagine this scenario: Henry Goode parks his car right in front of a parking attendant, whilst his disabled mother sits in the passenger seat. In full view of the attendant, he gets his mother's wheelchair out of the car boot, unfolds it and helps his mother into the wheelchair.

He says to the parking attendant, 'I'm just going to take my mother across the road'. Then he wheels her across the road to a friend's house under the watchful gaze of the parking attendant.

When Henry returns to his car he finds the parking attendant attaching a ticket to the windscreen. The parking attendant refuses to discuss the matter or to cancel the ticket. Henry appeals to the council, but the council was adamant and only after a lengthy exchange of letters is the parking ticket cancelled.

DAYLIGHT ROBBERIES

It started off just like any other day for Fred Holt when he went to his local bank. But the ordinary day turned extraordinary when two masked men burst into the bank brandishing an axe and a machete. In the terrifying raid the robbers held a young cashier hostage and held an axe to her throat. Customers were forced to lie on the floor as staff were made to hand over cash to the robbers.

If being a victim of this horrifying event wasn't bad enough, 77-year-old Mr Holt had parked his car nearby, and by the time he had given a statement to police officers, his car had been there for 20 minutes longer than allowed.

Mr Holt was not worried because the police officers who interviewed him said that traffic wardens had been told about the raid and asked not to issue tickets.

However, when Mr Holt got back to his car he was astounded to find a £30 parking ticket pinned to his windscreen – the reason: overstaying his allowed time in the street.

There's always someone you can bank on in a time of crisis.

> PARKING GRACE PERIOD!
>
> In April 2015, Eric Pickles (now Sir Eric) the then Secretary of State at the Department of Communities and Local Government introduced legislation which gave motorists in England a ten-minute grace period in paid for council parking bays.
>
> The effect of the legislation is that no parking ticket can be issued until a ten-minute grace period has expired after your paid for parking ends.

Understand and Deliver

Compassion, understanding and generally being nice ... three traits not normally associated with some of the more unpleasant parking attendants we've encountered. Read on if you dare!

JOBSWORTH

When a motorist's wife had a fatal heart attack in the car you would expect him to get help and sympathy, not a parking ticket.

An elderly woman suffered cardiac arrest on her way to her doctor's surgery in north London. Her husband, who was driving, was forced to stop on a yellow line outside the surgery to call 999. He went with his dying wife in the ambulance as she was rushed to St Mary's Hospital in Paddington. Tragically, she was dead on arrival.

The distraught husband returned to the surgery in tears, only to find he had been given a £100 parking ticket, despite a doctor's notice on his windscreen explaining the emergency.

A nearby shop owner told the Evening Standard, 'When the wardens came along we told them what had happened.

But one issued a ticket anyway. I was absolutely stunned. He actually said: "It's not my problem, I've got a job to do."'

Some things are worth more than jobs.

ALL FIRED UP OVER PARKING TICKETS

If your house caught fire, you would get very hot under the collar if the firemen who came to rescue you got a parking ticket.

But that's exactly what happened in Northern Ireland: firemen were getting parking tickets on their personal vehicles whilst out attending fires. The problem started when parking attendants began issuing parking tickets to firemen's cars, which they had parked outside fire stations whilst on duty attending emergencies. With no parking spaces at the station, fire fighters were parking their cars nearby, so they could jump in the fire engines and get to the fire as quickly as possible.

Unfortunately, the tickets were burning a hole in the wardens' pockets. As the fire engines dashed off to save lives and put the fires out, the wardens did their bit to make sure that everyone was all fired up on their return. As the Fire Brigades Union commented, for the fire- fighters to be told they could appeal against the fines was simply 'not good enough'.

YOUR PARKING FINES BEEN LIFT-ED

Your son is moving into a new flat. Would you go and help him? Of course you would.

But when one caring mother went to help her son move some boxes into his new flat little did she realise that this was to be the start of a real drama. During the move the lift got jammed between floors and the unfortunate lady was stuck for 18 hours until 2 pm the following day.

As the building was empty at the time, her cries for help were not heard. You can imagine her relief when she was finally rescued - she was very, very thankful. But her relief turned to fury when she discovered that a policeman, unaware of her plight, had popped a £60 parking ticket on her car.

On hearing what had happened, the police cancelled the fine.

PARKING TICKET TAKES YOUR BREATH AWAY

If your child has an asthma attack it's frightening. When it happens in a car away from home it is even more frightening.

So, imagine one woman's anger when she was given a parking ticket after she had stopped to look after her son when he had an asthma attack. The incident happened when a mother in South London had to park on zigzag lines outside a school so she could help her four-year-old boy with his asthma inhaler.

When a parking attendant approached, she explained the situation but amazingly the parking attendant still gave her a parking ticket.

Memo to traffic warden: take a deep breath before acting.

ANOTHER FINE MESS

A young mother was waiting to park in a car park in Cheam Village, when the three-month-old daughter of a friend she was looking after started to choke and struggle for breath.

The woman pulled over in a vacant motorcycle bay, leaving the engine running and hurried to clear the baby's airway. When a traffic warden approached her car, she assumed he was coming to offer assistance.

Instead, she was flabbergasted to see him smack an £80 parking ticket on her car before walking away. The mother said: 'I tried to say, "Can you hold on a minute, I've got a baby choking here," But he just laughed and said, "Well that's your problem", before walking away.'

SAFETY LAST

Councils claim that parking rules are there to ease traffic flow and make roads safer for motorists and pedestrians.

But unfortunately, this was not the experience of the Silverdale School choir when they travelled to give a Christmas Carol concert.

Hastings Council had given their coaches a designated spot to park, but when the coaches arrived at the spot a council parking attendant told them to move on. Despite the driver carefully explaining that the council had given them express permission to park, the parking attendant was adamant ... they had to move. As a result, the nine and ten year olds had to cross a busy main road. Fortunately, a kindly police officer spotted the danger and helped the youngsters across the road.

A spokesperson for the council said such a mix-up would not happen again, telling the Hastings Observer, 'Our priority is obviously the safety of the children involved.'

Fa-la-la-la-la, la-la-la-la!

SCHOOL PLAY HAS UNHAPPY ENDING

As proud parents watched their children in the school Christmas play, little did they know that the final act would have a very unhappy ending.

The twist in the plot came when the parents arrived at their cars after the play – which had overrun – and were outraged to find that a council parking attendant had slapped parking tickets on their cars as they watched the play.

The parents had parked outside Tannery Drift First School, in Royston, where 11am to 12pm weekday parking restrictions were in force.

A school spokeswoman told the Cambridge Evening News: 'In the past, when the police were in charge, they would always come and see if it was a school event.' She added that if there was a school event the police would ask parents to move their vehicles and no parking tickets were issued. However, even when parents explained to the council's parking attendant why they were there it didn't help.

One outraged father said: 'The parking attendant wasn't showing great Christmas spirit, was he? We are all very angry about what happened and many of us will appeal the tickets.'

DOWN UNDER UNLOADING

Air travel is stressful, so when you drive to the airport it's a relief to unload your luggage and get on your way. But for one Australian motorist it wasn't.

Officials at Melbourne Airport threatened to take a one-armed man to court over a parking ticket for taking too long to unload luggage from his car. Stephen McKenzie-McHarg was told by one parking attendant that he could briefly park in a bus zone to unload his family's luggage. However, while he was doing so, another attendant came along and gave him a ticket.

A furious Mr McKenzie-McHarg told the Melbourne Herald Sun, 'I wasn't 30 seconds, but the next little fella threw the book at me. He's saying, "Get going, get going". I said: "Why don't you give me a hand?" Then he said: "I'm going to book you."'

Stephen refused to pay the fine and appealed. Although the airport authority states on its website that 'The wellbeing of disabled passengers and visitors at Melbourne Airport is of the highest priority', it surprisingly indicated it was considering pressing charges in court to recover the fine.

Strewth.

IT CAN GET WORSE

When he crashed his Rover into a wall after swerving to avoid a cyclist, Ben Orton thought things couldn't get worse, but they did.

He managed to move his car to a nearby single yellow line in Guest Road, Petersfield. The following day, Christmas Eve, he got an unexpected and unwanted Christmas present … a parking ticket.

The 'presents' didn't stop coming. Four days later Santa's little helpers delivered another parking ticket and the next day a third parking ticket magically appeared.

Surely Mr Orton's luck had to change. He changed the car's wheels and moved the car to Glisson Road, Petersfield, where his family live and parked it in a residents' bay. But Santa's generosity knew no bounds and on 5 January he received not one but another two parking tickets – the first for invalidating a parking permit by initially marking it with the wrong date and one four hours later after he removed the first ticket.

Ho, Ho ... oh.

LOVE THY NEIGHBOUR

It's no joke unloading heavy props for Sunday-school class, but the burden gets heavier when you get a parking ticket.

The Reverend Peter Hadden was unloading props from his van parked outside the Christian Centre Ministry on Belgrave Crescent, Edinburgh, on what he thought was a single yellow line. He had just stepped inside the church to call for volunteers to help him when, three minutes later, 'verily it came to pass' that he found a £30 parking ticket on his windscreen.

Central Parking System (CPS), the company which at the time was contracted by Edinburgh Council to issue tickets, said the rear end of Rev. Hadden's van was parked over double yellow lines.

Rev. Hadden told the Scotsman: 'I thought I would park as far away from the busy junction with Dean Bridge as possible, to make it safer. It turns out that my back wheels were encroaching on double yellow lines, but common sense tells you that I was safely parked away from the junction.'

(Legal note: you can wait on a single or a double yellow line to load or unload, unless there are double yellow 'blips' on the kerb which means no loading at any time. If there is a single yellow 'blip' this indicates you can load and unload but only outside the times shown by a sign which indicates the loading restrictions. Both the yellow blips and the signs must be present for the restrictions to be legal. If no days are indicated on the signs the restrictions are in force every day including Sundays and Bank Holiday. And once you have finished you must move your vehicle.)

YOUR FIRST WEDDING PRESENT

It was a happy day for newlyweds Lorraine Lowe and husband Jason. The handsome couple had just left the registry office to find their first wedding present ... a bright yellow parking ticket.

Lorraine and Jason were waiting to have their photos taken when they spotted that specially selected gift ... a parking ticket on one of the bridal cars.

What was so upsetting was that town hall staff had authorised the wedding car to park in a bay outside the building. Not only that, but the car had been ticketed whilst the couple were getting married despite a notice in the windscreen saying: 'wedding party – bride and groom'.

Lorraine and Jason appealed against the parking ticket issued by Wigan Council's contractors and subsequently received a letter stating that 'after careful consideration of the mitigating circumstances' it was scrapping the parking fine. If only there'd been a bit of careful consideration in the first place.

O BROTHER WHERE PARKED THOU?

Blood donors save lives – just watch the ads on TV – but some get 'rewards' they don't deserve.

When former Royal Scot medic Gordon Bruce got an emergency call from his blood-donor centre saying there was a potential shortfall of his rare O positive blood type, Gordon immediately arranged an appointment and motored to Edinburgh. This was a thirty-mile journey he had regularly made every six months for the last 15 years but because of the possible shortfall in supplies, this journey was extremely important.

On his visit to the donor centre, Gordon was kept behind by staff because they could not stop him bleeding. As a result, he couldn't get back to his car before the pay-and- display ticket expired.

When he got back he found that the car had been parked six minutes after his time expired – or just 60 seconds after the five-minute grace period awarded to all motorists. Gordon immediately lodged an appeal but amazingly the council rejected his claim. Then the blood-donor centre wrote to the council to exercise a 'sense of goodwill and fairness' but Gordon heard nothing until a local newspaper stepped in. Surprise, surprise, within hours of the newspaper contacting the council, they cancelled the £60 fine.

CONGRATULATIONS! IT'S A PARKING TICKET

The joy of attending your child's birth is unforgettable, but for one new father it was doubly unforgettable.

Father-to-be Richard Evans drove to the Royal Shrewsbury Hospital in anticipation of the birth of his son. He parked in the car park and put £4 into the parking machine to cover what he thought was two days' parking before he went into the maternity unit. However, when after his son's birth he returned to his car the following day he was flabbergasted to find a parking ticket on the windscreen.

It is understood that the newborn left a statement in his nappy.

NO COUNCIL SUPPORT FOR DUNDEE SUPPORTERS

When a group of disabled Dundee football fans went to Dens Park to enjoy a day out to watch their favourite team they looked forward to a relaxing day of great football. But it was not to be.

Their specially adapted minibus arrived for the match, but the driver could not find a parking space even though he drove around the stadium. The minibus was spotted by a friendly police officer. He could see that the passengers were disabled people, including a wheelchair user and others with mobility difficulties, and offered to move some traffic cones so the bus could park safely.

Although the minibus clearly displayed a disabled badge, when they got back after the match, they found that a parking attendant had slapped a parking ticket on the minibus.

The group sent an appeal against the fine to Dundee City Council who, amazingly, rejected it. The group wanted to appeal again, but paid the fine as they were concerned that the penalty would increase. The group's plight was discovered by Dee4Life and the Dundee Supporters' Association agreed to pay the fine. They also offered the group a chance to return and watch Dundee in a future match for free.

As for the match itself, Dundee lost 3–1 to Gretna. But it was Dundee Council that scored a shameful own goal.

(Legal note: It pays to appeal against an unfair parking ticket straight away, and certainly within 14 days. All but the most miserly of councils will freeze the penalty charge whilst the appeal is being considered – even if the ticket says the charge doubles if not paid within 14 days. However, councils are happy to consider the payment of a parking fine as an admission of guilt. Thereafter, there is no recourse for appeal. The lesson is: Appeal NOW!)

Bending the Rules

Rules are meant to be broken, as Hollywood action film stars keep pointing out. But unlike our cinematic cousins, parking-ticket attendants very rarely play the hero ...

YOU NEED THE POWER OF PROPHECY

A motorist got a parking ticket for illegally parking whilst parked next to an illegible parking restrictions sign from which all the letters had fallen off.

Initially the council said that the sign was perfectly clear, but when photographs were submitted and the council were asked to read the signs themselves, they eventually cancelled the ticket.

LAND GRAB

If your family had parked on the same plot of derelict land for 40 years with no problem, you, too, would be surprised if you suddenly got a parking ticket.

Tom Sales, a retired bank manager, had lived in the same North London street since 1964. He and his neighbours regularly parked their cars on a disused piece of grass between the pavement and the wall of a nearby cemetery. But then out of the blue Mr Sales' car got a parking ticket after his son parked the car there. His son was taking some groceries into Mr Sales' house when the warden struck.

Mr Sales said, 'My son could not have been in the house any more than five minutes. When he went out, there was no one in sight. The warden must have put the ticket on and run off.'

Mr Sales appealed, with the support of three neighbours. Barnet Council refused to look at the land, saying that they 'are not prepared to enter into a debate' and that the penalty was issued correctly.

OK, so ... why wasn't one issued forty years ago?

DAYLIGHT ROBBIE-RY

Robbie Williams is well known for singing 'Let Me Entertain You' but some Leeds residents were far from entertained by the council's behaviour at one of his concerts.

Robbie's concert in Leeds last year was great for his fans but local residents claim a council cock-up meant that residents were incorrectly given police fines – for parking outside their own homes!

Robbie's first concert in Roundhay Park took place on a Friday night but on Saturday afternoon many residents who were parked outside their homes were given parking tickets because they weren't notified of any parking restrictions.

One resident, Kristine Longstaff, who was fined whilst parked outside her home, told the Yorkshire Evening News, 'I just thought – you have got to be joking! There was no notification, there was nothing on the car to warn me to move my car or get a parking ticket.'

West Yorkshire Police blamed a breakdown in communication with Leeds Council, and said that the council should have provided them with details of the cars already parked when the traffic cones were put out.

Suggestions that the traffic wardens shouted 'Take that!' as they issued the tickets were made up by me to finish the entry with a joke.

HEDGING THEIR BETS

We all go out for a drive to visit friends, but when John Carpenter and Darren Jones went to visit friends they were in for a very nasty shock.

When they got back to their car they were surprised to see a parking ticket claiming that they had parked in a restricted parking bay that was only available from 10 am to 4 pm. John and Darren looked everywhere for parking signs but couldn't see any.

They came back the next day and took photos of the parking bay and the photos clearly showed that there were no signs. They appealed to the council who refused the appeal, saying that the signs were clearly visible and clearly marked, despite the photographs submitted.

When they got the letter John and Darren went back to the spot and to their absolute amazement found that the council had cut down a hedge and there behind the hedge was a sign restricting the parking hours.

TWISTED LOGIC

Ever had an incorrect parking ticket? Would you expect the council that knows the parking ticket is incorrect to tell you? Well, you would be wrong!

Barnet Council was one council that didn't. This became clear after they incorrectly issued a parking ticket to Michael Dickson's car in Brampton Grove in Hendon. There were no parking restrictions in the morning when Mr Dickson parked his car. But when later that same day he got back to his car, he found a yellow line had been painted up to his car and a parking ticket slapped on his windscreen. Mr Dickson appealed against the ticket and a red-faced Barnet Council admitted they had made a mistake and cancelled the fine.

Surprisingly, however, the council said it would not be contacting other people who had also been unfairly ticketed, claiming they didn't know the names and addresses of the car owners. At the same time, they admitted that when fines are not paid the council sends letters to motorists' home addresses ... which are obtained from the DVLA. A council spokesperson claimed that the council only had the power to get people's addresses from the DVLA if they had not paid the initial fine.

So, if the council fines you incorrectly they won't write to tell you, but if you don't pay that same incorrect fine they write to you to pay up.

Makes perfect sense!

JUDGMENT OF SOLOMON

You say you parked correctly – the traffic warden says you didn't. How do you resolve the matter?

On the Greek island of Lesvos, they found a unique solution. When Petros Kakasavelis double-parked his car near the island's harbour, he returned to his vehicle to see a dreaded parking ticket. But when he examined it closely he was intrigued to find he had been charged for just half of a full parking ticket.

When he asked for an explanation, he was told that his vehicle was parked over a road marker which divided the jurisdiction areas of the port and traffic police and was therefore only charged for half a parking ticket.

Mr Kakasavelis was quoted as saying, 'I'm glad they didn't also bring a tow truck to haul half my car away.'

MYSTERY OF THE MOVING PARKING BAY

One day, Hendon resident Przemek Graszkiewicz dis- played his parking permit and left his car in a designated parking bay, as usual. When he got back a few days later he discovered that the council had moved his parking bay 'just like that', without giving advance notice to residents.

Imagine Mr Graszkiewicz's disbelief when he found that not only had the bay been moved to another spot on the road, but yellow lines had been painted around his car and a £40 parking ticket had materialised on his windscreen.

Mr Graszkiewicz complained in writing to the council. First, he was told that his letter had been received, then that it had got lost and he would have to resend it. Despite the fact that they had received Mr Graszkiewicz's original appeal they sent him another demand, this time for £80, claiming that he had not appealed against or paid the initial fine. Eventually, after another three months, the council telephoned Mr Graskiewicz to apologise for its mistake and to confirm it had cancelled the ticket.

The council moves in mysterious ways, but not as mysteriously as Mr Graszkiewicz's parking bay!

SLOW, SLOW, QUICK, QUICK, GO!

One lady, who had been parked in a side-turning off a busy shopping street, learned a very the hard parking ticket lesson.

The only way to drive out of the side road was to reverse out of it. She was finding this manoeuvre so difficult that she asked her partner to get out of the car and direct traffic.

A parking attendant with lightning-quick reflexes placed a parking ticket on her windscreen while she was waiting for her partner to come back to the car.

She told appealnow.com, 'The parking attendant issued me with a parking ticket whilst I was waiting for the busy road to clear before I could drive out. He quickly took a photo of the ticket he placed on the windscreen whilst I was slowly reversing on to the road at my partner's directions. I am sure the picture he snapped will show me sitting in my car.'

PRESTO-CHANGE-O!

For years, Howard Mitchell had parked his car in the same resident's bay without any problems. Just imagine his astonishment when he was given a ticket for parking in that very same space.

The ticket had been issued after parking attendants spotted a brand-new parking sign in the London Borough of Islington. The sign stated that the bay was no longer for residents' use and was available only for business parking. Only one problem: no rule change had been made and the sign should not have been put up in the first place! What was worse, Islington Council seemed unaware of its own blunder until Mr Mitchell appealed against his parking ticket.

A spokesperson for the Council said: 'We made a mistake and we apologise for any inconvenience caused. The error will be corrected within the next week and we will make every effort to ensure this doesn't happen again.'

PSYCHIC PARKING TICKETS

A motorist was surprised to find that she had received a parking fine before the time she had paid for expired. The accusation came after a driver was fined for parking in Harlow Road, High Wycombe, despite buying a ticket and returning to her car an hour early.

Andrew Knight said that his wife was 'astonished' to find a parking fine slapped on the windscreen even though his wife had bought a four-hour parking ticket. Mr Knight told the Bucks Free Press, 'She found a parking fine with a very feeble excuse that the contractors had reasonable cause to think she would be staying longer than the four hours for which she paid.' The council, however, denied that this happened.

Mr Knight commented 'How they came to that conclusion is beyond me. They do not, I believe, have special powers to see into the future. They are just trying to book as many people as possible.'

WE SHALL NOT BE MOVED

It all started off quietly when a motorist had his car moved so that Ealing Council contractors could paint yellow lines. But this simple matter started a chain reaction which came back to haunt him 14 months later.

Mike Fox's nightmare started when he was legally parked in a resident's parking bay, for which he had a permit. His car was moved and left in front of someone's drive. He was then given a parking ticket, and two days later found a message on his answering machine from Parking Services saying that British Telecom had moved his car and it was blocking someone's drive!

Mr Fox immediately wrote to Ealing Parking Services to complain about his ticket, but amazingly was told he would still have to pay the fine. He sent two more letters, and when he did not get any replies he assumed that the ticket had been cancelled. But ten months later he received a letter stating that the penalty still stood. The council was generous enough to concede that he could appeal against the decision, despite the lapse of time!

Eventually, after much to-ing and fro-ing, an embarrassed Ealing Council informed Mr Fox that the matter was closed. About time too.

A SLAP-HAPPY TICKET CHAPPY

Imagine you were feeding coins into a pay-and-display machine and you received a parking ticket before the machine printed the voucher. Would you be annoyed? You bet.

Roger Sailes parked his van, went to the back of the vehicle to find some change and walked to the pay-and- display machine, all of which took less than two minutes. Sadly, he attracted the attention of a parking attendant who can only be described as slap-happy. He stood next to Mr Sailes as he put money into the machine, then slapped a ticket on his windscreen before he had the chance to place the voucher on his vehicle.

When Mr Sailes confronted the man, he alleged the warden said to him, 'Who will they believe, you or me?'

Eventually, following inquiries by the local newspaper, the council climbed down and said it would cancel the parking ticket and look into Mr Sailes' complaint about the parking attendant's conduct.

IS NOWHERE SAFE?

If you park in your own private car park you'd expect your car to be safe from getting a ticket, wouldn't you? So, when a church volunteer in Lancashire parked in her church's private car park, she left her car without a qualm.

However, when she got back to her car she was distressed to find that a parking attendant had entered the private car park and left a parking ticket on her car. The parking ticket was eventually cancelled after an appeal was sent to the council telling them that the church car park was private and was not covered by the on-street parking laws.

Above the Law

Some councils, individuals and organisations believe that they are above the law. Well, when it comes to parking tickets they're just like the rest of us ...

AVOID A TICKET – BECOME A DIPLOMAT

How do you escape parking tickets? The answer: join the diplomatic service.

Many foreign diplomats in the UK have been dodging parking fines because generous parking rules often allow them to park on single yellow lines at any time, unlike the rest of us.

This policy differs from many other European capitals and US cities.

Consul Generals in Edinburgh are also permitted to leave their cars, which have special licence plates, in pay-and- display bays free of charge.

This official policy, which allows them to escape the fines handed out to ordinary drivers, makes Edinburgh more liberal than any other European capital, where fines are handed out regardless of who owns the vehicle.

Even though parking tickets cannot be legally enforced in court because of diplomatic immunity, failure to pay can sometimes mean that the diplomat is asked to leave by the host country.

COUNCIL(LOR) OF IMPERFECTION

Who wouldn't want to have their parking tickets cancelled? Michael Ross did. In fact, the Boston City Councillor had 35 parking tickets cancelled. Unfortunately for him he broke the law in doing so and was fined $2,000 by the State Ethics Commission.

The city allows Councillors to cancel parking tickets they receive, but only when they are received while on city business. Ross had received his citations, which carried about $1,000 in fines, between January 2002 and February 2006 for violations including failure to pay parking-meter fees and parking in resident-only spaces without a resident parking permit. Ross had 105 tickets dismissed, but the commission found that he was not working when he received 35 of them.

City officials confirmed that Ross has since reimbursed the city $1,000 for the parking fines.

DIPLOMATIC SOLUTION

More than 10 years ago New York City had a unique solution to the problem of diplomats who didn't pay their parking tickets? For many years New York authorities were frustrated by diplomats and their employees who flouted every parking restriction, then refused to pay millions of dollars a year in parking fines, claiming 'diplomatic immunity'.

However, the city adopted a cunning plan. First, they reduced the number of parking spaces allocated to each mission and consulate. Then they announced that diplomats would lose their diplomatic licence plates if they did not pay at least 60 per cent of their outstanding debt.

A spokesman for the New York Department of Finance said that following the announcement diplomats had received only 1,740 tickets, compared with the 161,053 issued in the five years before the change in policy.

Without their immunity, diplomats seemed suddenly to have caught a cold.

FINE PARKING!

How would you like it if you had to pay not only your own parking tickets, but also someone else's?

In Australia, taxpayers discovered that they had paid parking tickets for two ministers: New South Wales MPs Kerry Hickey, the Local Government Minister, and John Della Bosca, the Special Minister for State. The parking tickets had been paid out of their offices' budgets.

Mr Hickey had not paid a $70 infringement notice issued to him while he was attending a work-related function in December 2004. Mr Della Bosca got his parking fine in May 2004 for leaving his car in a no-parking zone. Under an exceedingly generous policy outlined in a memorandum from the Premier's

Department on Traffic Infringements, neither man was required to pay the fines. But wait! What's this? Government ministers doing a U- turn following a public outcry?

A spokesman for both ministers told the Australian Daily Telegraph that the ministers would repay the money to the government out of their own pockets. He added that there had been a mix-up between Mr Della Bosca and his driver.

So that's the mix-up between taxpayers' money and private responsibility sorted, then.

BADGE OF DISHONOUR

Parking attendants in Edinburgh are called 'Enforcers' because they are supposed to enforce parking regulations. One 'Enforcer', however, took a slightly more liberal view ... at least when it came to his own conduct.

Sabir Ali was supposed to ticket motorists who misused disabled badges, but used his mother's disability badge to park for free. And where did he park? Only at his employers, Central Parking Systems' headquarters in Edinburgh's Fountainbridge area!

When he was caught, Ali was suspended immediately, then fired after a disciplinary hearing. He admitted the scam, but complained that he shouldn't have been fired.

'I didn't think using the badge was that serious,' Ali told the Daily Record. 'I was pretty unlucky to get caught.'

Ali even had the cheek to appeal against his sacking, but was notified that the decision stood. 'We take blue badge misuse very seriously,' said a spokeswoman for Central Parking Systems.

One of Ali's colleagues, who did not want to be named, added, 'It is this sort of thing that gives wardens a bad name. We are told to watch out for misuse of disabled badges when we are out on patrol. So, for him to use his mum's to park his car for free is shocking.'

MAYOR DISCOVERS BEER FESTIVAL IS JUST THE TICKET

There were red faces at Woking Borough Council when it emerged that the mayor's official car had been caught in a compromising position.

When residents arrived at the Woking Beer Festival one Saturday evening in November 2006, who should they spot parked in a space reserved for disabled drivers? Their mayor's official chauffeur-driven car!

At the end of his visit, the mayor returned to the car to find that a parking attendant employed by his own council had whacked a parking ticket on the car.

'It is rather embarrassing,' he told the local News and Mail. 'In the past the leisure centre has provided the space for the mayor's car and I am now told it is to be removed and turned into a disabled bay. It's silly because in the mayoral car you really need to be as close as possible.'

To round off the evening somebody had also stolen the mayor's official pennant from the front of the car!

THE WORST NON-PAYER

Ten years ago, White Plains Council in the USA was owed a whacking $111,463 in unpaid parking tickets. Can you guess who the main culprit is? An errant motorist? A very forgetful motorist?

No. The astonishing answer is that the worst non-payer was the US government which owes the amazing figure. The parking-ticket dodgers were all federal public servants. Even the FBI and Secret Service agents are amongst the culprits together with postal employees, military recruiters and similar employees. Between them they managed to rack up 2,237 parking tickets in just 18 months, and what's more they had not paid any of them.

Remarkably the Federal Government owed more than four times as much in fines as the next culprit on the list.

BITING THE HAND THAT FEEDS

Birmingham residents had long complained of traffic warden 'hit squads'. In vain, until one year when they 'hit' City Transport Chief John Tyrrell, the man responsible for hiring the city's parking contractors.

Councillor Tyrrell and his colleagues were attending a board meeting at the Beta First centre in Hockley Hill when the parking posse struck. Five wardens in a white minibus swooped on the area just after 8 pm and issued dozens of tickets. When the raid was discovered, the meeting was suspended and people rushed to their cars – too late. Over 30 community leaders ended up with parking tickets, including Mr Tyrrell.

When asked to comment, he said: 'It does seem strange that a team of wardens turned up just at that time.'

Gleeful onlookers noted the poetic justice of Mr Tyrrell's own wardens slapping him with a parking ticket.

One resident told the local press, 'You've got to laugh haven't you. The council has denied there are hit squads, but now they have the proof first hand.'

TRUST ME, I'M A JUDGE

What would you do if you owed $12,000 in unpaid parking tickets?

A former administrative law judge for the Parking Violations Bureau in the US came up with a unique scheme for his 167 parking tickets. Only one problem: the scheme was dishonest!

The State Supreme Court's Appellate Division suspended the judge after a disciplinary committee found that he used his knowledge of the Bureau to avoid paying the summonses over two years.

First, he didn't turn in his ID card when he left the Parking Violations Bureau, and displayed it on his dashboard to discourage traffic agents from giving him tickets. Then he ordered vanity license plates for his two cars, both using combinations of numbers and letters that he knew would give him a technical defence against any summons issued. Finally, the former judge left papers and other objects on his dashboard to obscure a sticker code that would indicate the vehicle had vanity plates, preventing its proper identification.

Despite his best efforts, in the space of two years the judge had incurred $12,000 in unpaid parking summonses, not including late fees that could not be assessed because of his evasive techniques.

The judge's parking-ticket dodge was clever, but he was also clever enough to know when to quit: in the end he settled with the Parking Violations Bureau for $8,225, a handsome 30 per cent discount on the full figure he owed.

CREDITS

The stories in this book have been compiled from the many thousands of emails people have sent to my website www.appealnow.com.

Without them, and their concern for parking justice, this book would never have been made possible. Thank you.

About the Author

BARRIE SEGAL is an Amazon Number 1 Author, a broadcaster and Chartered Accountant and a qualified accountant and broadcaster. He is the founder of the parking ticket websites www.ParkingTicketExpert.com and www.AppealNow.com.

Richard Hammond of "Top Gear" fame called him "The U.K's leading parking ticket expert," and he certainly lives up to that title, regularly appearing on television and radio and in the press advising motorists on how to fight their unfair parking tickets.

He has reviewed more than 60,000 parking tickets and been involved in more than 7,000 appeals to the Parking Adjudicator tribunal. He also represented the motorist in the High Court case of "Moses -v- Barnet" and won a stunning victory which led to some £300 million of parking tickets being declared illegal.

He is the author of "The Parking Ticket Awards: Crazy Councils, Meter Madness & Traffic Warden Hell" which chronicles the astoundingly crazy parking tickets issued in the U.K. and the rest of the world.

His most recent book parking ticket book is "Barrie Segal's Quick Guide To Fight Your Parking Ticket" which is based on his 14 years of experience fighting parking tickets on behalf of motorists.

For more than 45 years he has advised companies on how to be more efficient and profitable, with a particular speciality in advising law firms. In that time, he has lectured extensively on business matters and is also much in demand as an after-dinner speaker. Based on his years of knowledge and experience he continues to coach clients on how to speak effectively in public.

He is the author of The 5 Great Myths of Public Speaking! and the "Zero To Hero Public Speaking Secrets" course. He also runs one-to-one and group coaching courses on Public Speaking.

Based on his business experience, he written books on how to minimise and do away with the stress of various aspects of people's home and business life including,

Financial Ratios Analysis: A "How to" Guide to Learn The Three Key Accounting Ratios for Management of Your Company Performance For Business Owners and Internet Marketers

Break-Even Analysis: A How to Guide to Learn Break-Even Analysis in Less Than 1 hour!

The Joy of Tidying Paperwork: The Easy 7 Step Secret to Tidy and Sort Your Paperwork!

He is a former member of The Magic Circle and is a keen exponent of Tai Chi.

Find out more at Barries Author page at amzn.to/2AMYFEV

Books and Courses by Barrie Segal

Zero To Hero Public Speaking Secrets

The 5 Great Myths of Public Speaking!

Barrie Segal's Quick Guide To Fight Your Parking Ticket

Break-Even Analysis: A How to Guide to Learn Break-Even Analysis in Less Than 1 hour!

Financial Ratios Analysis: A "How to" Guide to Learn The Three Key Accounting Ratios for Management of Your Company Performance For Business Owners and Internet Marketers

The Joy of Tidying Paperwork: The Easy 7 Step Secret to Tidy and Sort Your Paperwork!

To be the first to know when these books will be published and to get your free bonuses go to barriesegal.com/crazyparkingticketawards.html or bit.ly/barriesegal

Can I Ask A Favour?

If you enjoyed this book, found it useful or otherwise then I'd really appreciate it if you would post a short review on Amazon. I do read all the reviews personally so that I can continually write what people are wanting.

If you'd like to leave a review then please visit the "My Review" area.

Thanks for your support!

Printed in Great Britain
by Amazon